ARMIN A. BROTT

*The* ███████ ███████ *Father*
*The* ██████ *Guide for Da* ███ *Be*

"For fathers soon expecting the ultimate gift—a new member of the family—*The Expectant Father* is his best friend."
—CNN Interactive

"One would be hard put to find a question about having a baby that's not dealt with here, all from the father's perspective."
—*Library Journal*

*The New Father:*
*A Dad's Guide to the First Year*

"This book would make a great gift for any new dad."
—Lawrence Kutner, Ph.D., columnist, *Parents* magazine

ARMIN A. BROTT

FAQ FOR
**NEW**
FATHERS

Abbeville Press Publishers
NEW YORK   LONDON

EDITOR: Will Lach
COPY EDITOR: Sharon Lucas
DESIGNER: Misha Beletsky
TYPESETTER: Ada Rodriguez
PRODUCTION MANAGER: Louise Kurtz

ISBN 978-0-7892-1270-2

Library of Congress Cataloguing-in-Publication Data available upon request

For bulk and premium sales and for text adoption procedures, write to Customer Service Manager, Abbeville Press, 116 West 23rd Street, New York, NY 10011, or call 1-800-ARTBOOK.

Visit Abbeville Press online at www.abbeville.com.

# CONTENTS

# INTRODUCTION

I have been a new father several times. The first time I became a new father—and to be honest, even after that first time—I was full of questions. (A new baby can do funny things to your memory.)

In my search for the "right" answers, I did research in libraries and on the web, and I interviewed academics and fatherhood researchers. But perhaps most importantly, I talked to lots of other new dads—some with one child under their belt, others who had done it many times before. Most of them had questions similar to mine.

My passion for finding answers led to my first book, *The Expectant Father*, and the success of that book led to my second title, *The New Father*. Over the years, I've heard from thousands of dads (and moms), and while they still crave information about those basic questions, some people want their answers in small, easily digestible chunks. That's why we created this series of FAQ books. Our goal is simple: to give you straightforward, solid answers to your most pressing questions, but in a fun, entertaining way that will help you retain the information so you can put it to use right away or recall it later on, whenever the need arises. Our test readers have loved this approach and we're confident that you will, too.

—Armin Brott
2016

WEEK

1

Right from birth, your baby is capable of making a number of _____ .

   **a.** mathematical calculations
   **b.** intellectual decisions
   **c.** expressions
   **d.** mistakes

b. Right from birth, your baby is capable of making a number of **intellectual decisions**.

She can't, however, differentiate herself from the other objects in her world. If she grasps your hand, for example, her little brain doesn't know whether she's holding her own hand or yours—or, for that matter, that those things on the ends of her arms even belong to her.

TIP It's fascinating to watch how your baby deals with new information and how her brain develops.

At this point, most of the vocal sounds your baby produces will be cries or _____ grunts, snorts, and squeaks.

    **a.** soft
    **b.** infuriating
    **c.** animal-like
    **d.** loud

c. At this point, most of the vocal sounds your baby produces will be cries or **animal-like** grunts, snorts, and squeaks.

When he hears a noise or a voice—especially your partner's or yours—he'll become quiet and try to focus.

TIP Say, "Hey, baby," or something else, and there's a good chance that he'll turn his head toward you.

During the first week after the baby is born, your partner may feel relief that _____ .

a. college is years away
b. the pregnancy is finally over
c. she married you
d. you're not running for Congress

A

b. During the first week after the baby is born, your partner may feel relief that **the pregnancy is finally over.**

She may also feel a deep need to get to know the baby, feel impatience at her lack of mobility, and worry about how she'll perform as a mother and whether she'll be able to breast-feed.

TIP Help out as much as you can. As her confidence builds over the next few weeks, those worries should disappear.

---

"Engrossment" describes "a father's sense of absorption, preoccupation, and interest in his _____ ."

   **a.** job
   **b.** beer
   **c.** hobbies
   **d.** baby

d. "Engrossment" describes "a father's sense of absorption, preoccupation, and interest in his **baby**."

Dr. Martin Greenberg coined the term in the 1970s. So what exactly triggers it in men? Exactly the same thing that prompts similar nurturing feelings in women: early contact with their infants.

TIP Take a deep breath and do what feels most natural to you—chances are it'll be exactly the right thing.

Almost all new dads immediately look for_____ between themselves and their baby.

    **a.** conflict
    **b.** physical similarities
    **c.** psychological connection
    **d.** telepathy

# A

b. Almost all new dads immediately look for **physical similarities** between themselves and their baby.

For most of us—regardless of how many prenatal appointments we go to, how many times we hear the baby's heartbeat, feel her kick, or see her squirm on an ultrasound—the baby isn't completely "real" until after the birth, when we finally meet each other face-to-face.

TIP Don't feel bad—after you've counted those fingers and toes, check to see whether the baby has your chin.

About 1 in 1,000 healthy babies
and 2 in 100 in intensive care
units have _____ .

**a.** a valid driver's license
**b.** hearing loss
**c.** green eyes
**d.** 6 fingers

b. About 1 in 1,000 healthy babies and 2 in 100 in intensive care units have hearing loss.

If the loss is caught during newborn screenings, babies can be fitted with hearing aids that can help prevent speech and language problems.

TIP The tests are safe, quick, and painless. In fact, babies usually sleep right through them.

Within the first hour of life, most healthy infants have a period of _____ that lasts an average of 40 minutes.

- **a.** giggles
- **b.** incessant crying
- **c.** quiet alertness
- **d.** confusion

c. Within the first hour of life, most healthy infants have a period of **quiet alertness** that lasts an average of 40 minutes.

Babies in quiet-alert mode rarely move—all their energy is channeled into seeing, hearing, and absorbing information about their new world.

TIP This is a great time to just watch. Babies can (and do) follow objects with their eyes and may even imitate your facial expressions. That's when it'll first hit you that there's a real person inside that tiny body.

_____ is a perfectly natural—and for some babies, frequent—state.

**a.** Crying
**b.** Peeing
**c.** Sleeping
**d.** Giggling

A

a. **Crying** is a perfectly natural—and for some babies, frequent—state.

Crying is not a bad thing—it not only allows the baby to communicate but also provides valuable exercise.

TIP Often just picking him up and walking around with him will stop the crying. It turns out that what makes babies stop crying is not being upright, but the movement that gets them there.

In their first week or so of life, most babies lose some weight— often as much as \_\_\_\_\_ of their birth weight.

    **a.** 30%
    **b.** 18%
    **c.** 2%
    **d.** 10%

d. In their first week or so of life, most babies lose some weight—often as much as 10% of their birth weight.

This can be pretty scary, especially since babies are generally supposed to get bigger over time, not smaller.

———

TIP This shrinking baby thing is perfectly normal (in the first few days the baby isn't eating much), and your baby will probably regain her birth weight by the time she's 2 weeks old.

Half of a baby's sleep time is spent in quiet sleep, the other half in \_\_\_\_ .

    **a.** tears
    **b.** even quieter sleep
    **c.** waiting to pounce
    **d.** active sleep

# A

d. Half of a baby's sleep time is spent in quiet sleep, the other half in **active sleep**.

The baby may smile or frown, make sucking or chewing movements, and even whimper or twitch—just as adults do in our active sleep state.

TIP If your sleeping baby starts to stir, fuss, or seems to be waking up unhappy, wait a few seconds before you pick him up to feed, change, or hold him. Left alone, he may well slip back into the quiet sleep state.

By the time your baby _____ ,
you'll have changed about
10,000 diapers.

   **a.** has graduated from
        college
   **b.** gets potty-trained
   **c.** learns French
   **d.** can sing

b. By the time your baby **gets potty-trained**, you'll have changed about 10,000 diapers.

But 10,000 is a ballpark figure. Boys will go through more diapers because they're usually potty trained later than girls. And of course, for twins or more, well, you can do the math.

---

TIP Never miss an opportunity to change a diaper. The quicker and more efficiently you learn to get the job done, the less time you'll have to spend doing it. Plus, it's actually a great bonding experience.

By about the fourth day after birth, the ____ will be replaced with a much more pleasant-looking concoction.

   **a.** baby's vomit
   **b.** meconium
   **c.** regular hospital food
   **d.** diaper smoothie

b. By about the fourth day after the birth, the **meconium** will be replaced with a much more pleasant-looking concoction.

Meconium. That's the word for those greenish-black, sticky, tarry bowel movements that may have you worrying that there's something wrong with your baby's intestines.

TIP Fortunately, once the meconium is out of your baby's system, you won't have to deal with it again—at least until your next baby arrives.

Your baby's \_\_\_\_ will drop off
anywhere from 1 to 3 weeks
after she's born.

   **a.** IQ
   **b.** tail stump
   **c.** appetite
   **d.** umbilical-cord stump

A

_____

d. Your baby's **umbilical-cord stump** will drop off anywhere from 1 to 3 weeks after she's born.

Folding down the front of the diaper exposes the stump to more air and speeds up the falling-off process. Other than keeping the stump clean and dry, there's no need to do anything special to take care of it.

_____

TIP When it does fall off, a small amount of bleeding is normal.

_____, your partner isn't much better off than she is physically.

    **a.** Intellectually
    **b.** Psychologically
    **c.** Fiscally
    **d.** Emotionally

d. **Emotionally**, your partner isn't much better off than she is physically.

Now that the baby is really here, she may feel a lot of pressure to assume her new role as mother and to breast-feed properly.

———

TIP Be prepared. She's likely to be a little impatient at her lack of mobility. She'll probably experience the "baby blues," and may even suffer from post-partum depression.

Help your _____ resist the urge to do too much too soon.

**a.** partner
**b.** mother-in-law
**c.** baby
**d.** doctor

# A

a.  Help your **partner** resist the urge to do too much too soon.

She needs to rest. A lot. Anything you can do to help her do that will be good for her, good for your baby, and good for you.

---

TIP Take over the household chores, or ask someone else to help. Control the visiting hours and the number of people who can come at any given time. And above all, try to keep your sense of humor.

Don't expect your \_\_\_\_\_ to be
as excited as you are about the
birth of your baby.

    **a.** boss
    **b.** pets
    **c.** other children
    **d.** accountant

b. Don't expect your **pets** to be as excited as you are about the birth of your baby.

Many dogs and cats resent their new—and lower—status in the house. To minimize the trauma for your pet (and to minimize the chance your pet will do something to harm the baby), try to get your pet used to the baby as early as possible.

TIP You can do this even before the baby comes home by putting a blanket in the baby's bassinet in the hospital, then rushing it home to your pet.

Try to spend _____ every day
(in 5-minute installments)
doing something with the baby
one-on-one.

   **a.** no more than 10 minutes
   **b.** 5 or 6 hours
   **c.** as little time as possible
   **d.** at least 20 minutes

d. Try to spend **at least 20 minutes** every day (in 5-minute installments) doing something with the baby one-on-one.

Chatting, reading aloud, rocking, making faces, experimenting with the baby's reflexes, or even simply catching her gaze and looking into her eyes are great activities.

TIP Be encouraging, be gentle, and support the baby's head. Above all, take your cues from the baby—if she seems bored or fussy, stop what you're doing.

_____ is just about the best thing you can do for your child.

**a.** Breast-feeding
**b.** Quitting smoking
**c.** Training for a marathon
**d.** Teaching her to swim

## A

a. **Breast-feeding** is just about the best thing you (okay, actually your partner) can do for your child.

Breast milk provides exactly the right balance of nutrients your newborn needs. It also greatly reduces the chance that your baby will develop food allergies.

TIP You may not think you have much of a role to play in breast-feeding, but you do. The more supportive and encouraging you are, the longer your partner will breastfeed and the more she'll enjoy it.

You _____ burp your baby at the middle and the end of every feeding, more often if you feel it's necessary.

**a.** should not
**b.** should
**c.** may be afraid to
**d.** might not want to

b. You **should** burp your baby at the middle and the end of every feeding, more often if you feel it's necessary.

When babies drink—especially from bottles—they almost always swallow some air. Because they do most of that drinking on their side, the air gets trapped in their stomach. Sometimes babies burp on their own, but they usually need a little help.

TIP There's no right or wrong way to bring up a belch. Just make sure his head is higher than his butt and have a towel handy to clean up afterward.

MONTH

By the end of this month, he'll probably follow an object moving _____ by in front of him.

   **a.** vertically
   **b.** slowly
   **c.** excitedly
   **d.** quickly

b. By the end of this month, he'll probably follow an object moving **slowly** by in front of him.

Your baby is already expressing an interest in finding out what's going on in his world. He stares longer at new objects than familiar ones, and he loves high-contrast, black-and-white patterns and faces.

TIP As you're moving an object in front of him, send it behind something and see whether the baby continues moving his eyes to where he expects the object to reemerge.

As her vocal chords mature, your baby will expand her collection of ___ to include cooing noises.

  **a.** vintage vinyl
  **b.** random noises
  **c.** animal sounds
  **d.** Bee Gees

# A

c. As her vocal chords mature, your baby will expand her collection of **animal sounds** to include cooing noises.

She's already beginning to differentiate between language and the other kinds of noise she hears all day. She may respond to voices—especially your partner's and yours—by turning toward them.

TIP She really enjoys being spoken to. So chatter away!

He loves being held, rocked, and making _____ , and may stare intently at you for 15–20 seconds at a stretch.

    **a.** plans for the future
    **b.** bowel movements
    **c.** you nervous
    **d.** eye contact

A

d. He loves being held, rocked, and making **eye contact**, and may stare intently at you for 15-20 seconds at a stretch.

He's starting to form an emotional attachment and feelings of trust for the people who care for him.

TIP Pay close attention to how he reacts to what you're doing. He may cry as a way of demanding more attention or in protest at being overloaded with attention.

The sooner a dad has a chance to spend time with his _____ , the quicker the bonding process will start.

    **a.** new car
    **b.** chihuahua
    **c.** baby
    **d.** partner

c. The sooner a dad has a chance to spend time with his **baby**, the quicker the bonding process will start.

Generally speaking, men who attend their baby's birth bond slightly faster than those who don't.

TIP If you weren't able to be there for the birth, don't worry—not being there doesn't automatically interfere with attachment (and being there doesn't guarantee it).

Plenty of adoptive parents, particularly those who adopted _____ , feel a little insecure or inadequate.

**a.** on a whim
**b.** because of infertility
**c.** by mistake
**d.** twins

b. Plenty of adoptive parents, particularly those who adopted **because of infertility**, feel a little insecure or inadequate.

Studies of adoptive parents have shown that a majority feel some kind of love for their children right from the very first contact.

TIP So jump in. The sooner you hold your newly adopted baby, the sooner those feelings of love will work their way to the surface.

For about the first 6 to 8 weeks of life, your baby probably won't give you much _____ .

    **a.** love
    **b.** gas
    **c.** feedback
    **d.** trouble

A

c. For about the first 6 to 8 weeks of life, your baby probably won't give you much **feedback**.

She won't smile, laugh, or react to you in any noticeable way. In fact, just about all she'll do is cry. This can be really demoralizing.

TIP Get closer. There's a lot of evidence that parent-child bonding comes as a result of physical closeness. And be patient. If you spend time with your baby, you'll find lots of little opportunities to connect.

# 1 MONTH

At this age, you can read _____ to your baby.

    **a.** just about anything
    **b.** nothing but Shakespeare
    **c.** Klingon
    **d.** absolutely nothing

a. At this age, you can read **just about anything** to your baby.

The goal at this stage isn't to actually teach your baby anything; it's simply to get her used to the sounds and rhythms of language and to have her start associating reading with calm, quiet, and security.

TIP **Try to read to her every day and set up a regular time and place.**

---

Since your baby still isn't capable of grabbing or _____ much, he's doing most of his learning with his eyes.

- **a.** wrestling
- **b.** talking
- **c.** holding on to
- **d.** reading

c. Since your baby still isn't capable of grabbing or **holding on to** much, he's doing most of his learning with his eyes.

For the first few months, infants are particularly responsive to high contrast, so black-and-white toys and patterns are often a big hit.

TIP To stimulate your baby visually, fasten an unbreakable mirror securely to the inside of the crib, and make sure the baby has lots of different things to look at besides his own adorable face.

Yes, all that wild, seemingly random arm and leg flailing really has _____ .

    **a.** a purpose
    **b.** no possible purpose
    **c.** dangerous consequences
    **d.** great comedic potential

a. Yes, all that wild, seemingly random arm and leg flailing really has **a purpose**.

Understanding your baby's reflexes can give you greater insight into her behavior. They're also a lot of fun, for you as well as the baby.

TIP By keeping track of when reflexes appear and disappear, you'll be able to monitor your baby's development.

For about 10–20% of _____ , "baby blues" can develop into postpartum depression.

    **a.** older children
    **b.** new moms
    **c.** dads
    **d.** police officers

b. For about 10–20% of **new moms**, "baby blues" can develop into postpartum depression.

Sadly, a lot of moms who have postpartum depression don't get the assistance they need—often because they feel too embarrassed to admit to anyone else what they're feeling. Untreated, the depression can last for years.

TIP You know your partner better than anyone. If she starts doing or saying things that are out of character—like "I really hate this baby"—you'll have to get her the help she needs.

As natural as _____ is, a large
percentage of women have
some kind of difficulty with it.

    **a.** eating insects
    **b.** public nudity
    **c.** hunting
    **d.** breast-feeding

d. As natural as **breast-feeding** is, a large percentage of women have some kind of difficulty with it.

Breast-feeding problems range from stress and frustration to pain and infection. Women who have problems are far more likely to give up breast-feeding than those who don't.

TIP Be supportive and encouraging. Help her explore different feeding positions and make sure she's got something to eat and drink while nursing—it's very calorie-sapping and dehydrating. You have a big role to play here!

When a woman is breastfeeding, there's a risk that almost any _____ could get passed into her milk and affect the baby.

    **a.** drug she takes
    **b.** dance step she makes
    **c.** joke she cracks
    **d.** movie she watches

a. When a woman is breast-feeding, there's a risk that almost any **drug she takes** could get passed into her milk and affect the baby.

Most of the time the risk is very small, but sometimes it's not.

TIP Check out *Medications and Mothers' Milk* by Thomas W. Hale. The book (and website, medsmilk.com) is a comprehensive listing of prescription and nonprescription drugs, herbal remedies, and even illegal drugs, each evaluated for safety to both mother and baby during breast-feeding.

Starting at about 2 weeks of age,
\_\_\_\_\_ of babies develop colic,
crying spells that can last for
hours.

    **a.** 45–50%
    **b.** 100%
    **c.** 60–70%
    **d.** 10–20%

# A

d. Starting at about two weeks of age, **10–20%** of babies develop colic, crying spells that can last for hours.

Here are some things that may help you cope:
(1) Go to the drugstore.
(2) Tag-team crying duty.
(3) Hold the baby facing you. Put his head over your shoulder with your shoulder pressing on his stomach.
(4) Hold the baby a little less.
(5) Try swaddling.
(6) Don't take it personally.

# 1 MONTH

---

Handling your older children's reactions to their new sibling requires an extra touch of _____ .

    **a.** gentleness and sensitivity
    **b.** harsh discipline
    **c.** bribery
    **d.** class

A

a. Handling your older children's reactions to their new sibling requires an extra touch of **gentleness and sensitivity**.

Kids usually start out wildly excited by their new status as big brother or sister, but most will have some adjustment problems later on (anger, jealousy, tantrums, and even trying to hurt the baby).

TIP Make sure you get some private time with your older children, doing things that only big kids get to do (eating ice cream, playing catch, reading books, going to the movies).

2

MONTHS

As her brain develops, your baby will appreciate more _____ .

    **a.** computer code
    **b.** complex patterns
    **c.** classical music
    **d.** delicate flavors

b. As her brain develops, your baby will appreciate more complex patterns.

Toward the end of this month, she may begin to stare intently at very small items. She gets excited when she sees familiar objects, but still has some trouble with "object permanence" (which means that as far as the baby is concerned, anything she can't see simply doesn't exist).

# 2 MONTHS

And now, the moment you've been waiting for: your baby is finally able to _____ .

    **a.** walk
    **b.** feed herself
    **c.** do a somersault
    **d.** smile at you

d. And now, the moment you've been waiting for: your baby is finally able to smile at you.

Your baby will now start smiling in response to things that please her. (Sorry, but until now those things you thought were smiles were probably just gas.)

TIP Yet another in a long list of great reasons to keep your camera handy at all times. Those smiles are absolutely amazing. And there's nothing like having your baby smile at one of your jokes to make you feel like a great dad.

Most OB/GYNs advise their patients to refrain from intercourse for at least _____ after giving birth.

  **a.** 6 weeks
  **b.** 1 year
  **c.** 3 days
  **d.** 1 hour

a. Most OB/GYNs advise their patients to refrain from intercourse for at least 6 **weeks** after giving birth.

Resuming intercourse ultimately depends on the condition of your partner's cervix and vagina, and, more important, on how you're both feeling.

TIP Before you mark that date on your calendar, remember that the 6-week rule is only a guideline. Chances are it'll be a while longer than that. A long while.

When you do finally get around to making love, you should expect the first few times to be
_____ .

   **a.** earth-shattering
   **b.** disappointing
   **c.** a time of tentative
       rediscovery
   **d.** over really quickly

c. When you do finally get around to making love, you should expect the first few times to be **a time of tentative rediscovery**.

She may also be worried that having sex will hurt. You may be afraid of the same thing or that those extra pounds she hasn't lost yet will interfere with her pleasure.

TIP Go slowly, take your cues from her, and give yourselves plenty of time to get used to each other again.

She might want to _____ at a time when you're simply too tired to move.

    **a.** pick a fight
    **b.** break out in song
    **c.** cuddle
    **d.** make love

A

d. She might want to **make love** at a time when you're simply too tired to move.

Or you might want to have sex when she's feeling "touched out," having spent an entire day with a baby crawling all over her, sucking her breasts.

TIP Talking about sex can make some people uncomfortable. But at times like these, it's critical. The months right after the birth of a baby are a particularly vulnerable time for your sex life.

The first few \_\_\_\_\_ of fatherhood are riddled with fears.

   **a.** decades
   **b.** minutes
   **c.** months
   **d.** years

c. The first few **months** of fatherhood are riddled with fears.

Here are some of the most common: not being able to live up to your expectations, not being able to protect your children, not being ready to assume the role of father, not being able to love the baby enough, not being in control, being angry at your baby, and repeating the mistakes made by your own father.

---

TIP All new fathers are afraid sometimes. Anyone who claims fatherhood didn't bring out at least some fears is lying to you.

It's hard to admit, but like it or not, your baby is _____ .

    **a.** running your life
    **b.** smarter than you
    **c.** really annoying
    **d.** gorgeous

a. It's hard to admit, but like it or not, your baby is **running your life**.

You may be a great salesman, master negotiator, or cult leader, but your ability to turn adults to your way of thinking won't work with a baby.

---

TIP You've got a very Zen choice to make: you can either learn to accept change and bend, or you can break.

---

At this age, your baby has no business eating anything but
_____ .

    **a.** raw meat
    **b.** organic foods
    **c.** breast milk or formula
    **d.** Subway sandwiches

c. At this age, your baby has no business eating anything but **breast milk or formula**.

In the meantime, give the baby lots of different objects to put in his mouth. But be extremely careful that none of them has removable pieces or sharp edges, or is small enough to be a choking hazard.

———

TIP Anything that can fit through the tube in a standard roll of toilet paper is too small.

Your baby focuses best on objects that are _____ from her.

    **a.** 8–12 inches
    **b.** less than an inch
    **c.** snatched away
    **d.** 10–12 feet

a. Your baby focuses best on objects that are **8–12 inches** from her.

So be sure to hold toys and other objects within that range. Play tracking games, moving objects slowly back and forth in front of her eyes.

TIP You can also help boost her hand-eye coordination by holding an object within arm's reach and letting her try to grab it.

Expose the baby to as wide a variety of _____ as possible.

    **a.** zoo animals
    **b.** lighting conditions
    **c.** snakes
    **d.** smells, sounds, and textures

**A**

---

d. Expose the baby to as wide
   a variety of **smells, sounds,
   and textures** as possible.

Let your baby discover the smell
of flowers when you're out for
a walk, the sound of the radio
or any musical instruments you
have around the house, the feel
of the satin edge of his blanket.
But be very careful to make
sure that nothing ends up in his
mouth, that the sounds aren't
too loud (babies' hearing is very
sensitive and easily damaged),
and that you don't leave any
exploratory objects alone with
him.

Your baby should always sleep on _____ .

    **a.** Mars
    **b.** her back
    **c.** her tummy
    **d.** time

b. **Your baby should always sleep on her back.**

Until about 20 years ago, parents had always been told to put their babies to sleep on their tummy. The thinking was that if a baby sleeping on his back vomited, she'd aspirate the vomit and choke to death. Turns out that wasn't happening.

TIP This is serious stuff. Right after the recommendation changed from tummy sleeping to back sleeping, the incidence of sudden infant death syndrome (SIDS) went down by more than 40%.

Your baby's skull is made up of
_____ that will remain somewhat
flexible until she's 2.

    **a.** noodles
    **b.** opinions
    **c.** several bones
    **d.** sticks and stones

c. Your baby's skull is made up of **several bones** that will remain somewhat flexible until she's 2.

This is why babies who lie on their backs for too long (particularly preemies) may develop a flat spot on the skull. In most cases, this kind of "positional molding" isn't anything to worry about.

———

TIP If your baby's head looks asymmetrical or you think she's got a flat spot, the best thing to do is to frequently switch her sleeping positions.

In the past decade, there has been a lot of controversy about _____ .

   **a.** green tech
   **b.** immunizations
   **c.** Apple versus Android
   **d.** the housing bubble

b. There has been a lot of controversy lately about **immunizations**.

Today's vaccinations protect babies against almost a dozen diseases. Almost all public schools, and many private ones, require proof of vaccination before admitting a child. Most health experts agree that vaccinations—after clean water and flush toilets—are among the most important health advances in history. They're also quite safe. The initial claim that vaccines or their preservatives cause autism or other conditions was proved to be fraudulent.

Premature babies usually catch up to their age-mates by the time they're _____ .

**a.** six months
**b.** 4 feet tall
**c.** 2 or 3
**d.** married

c. Premature babies usually catch up to their age-mates by the time they're **2 or 3**.

But the more premature the baby, the longer it takes to pull even. To calculate what's normal development for a preemie, use her adjusted age (her actual age minus the number of months premature). So a four-month old baby who was born two months early should be evaluated against two-month-old standards.

Getting your home _____ is a process that never ends.

    **a.** remodeled
    **b.** clean
    **c.** scent-free
    **d.** childproofed

d. Getting your home **child-proofed** is a process that never ends.

Check out your baby's sleeping area. If you're worried that your baby will get cold, put her in a warm sleep suit—do *not* use blankets. If you've hung toys across the crib for the baby to swat at, make sure they are tied on very, very securely.

By the end of this month, your baby's _____ schedule should start to get a little more regular and predictable.

**a.** sleep and nap
**b.** exercise
**c.** work
**d.** visiting

# A

a. By the end of this month your baby's **sleep and nap** schedule should start to get a little more regular and predictable.

Chances are that his schedule will be exactly the opposite of what you'd hoped for: sleeping during the day and up at night. In a way, this makes sense. While she was pregnant, your partner was probably awake during the day, and all of her movements rocked the baby to sleep.

TIP Your mission, of course, will be to gradually reverse that schedule.

Some new _____ will want to be held the same way the baby is being held.

    **a.** neighbors
    **b.** fathers
    **c.** big brothers and sisters
    **d.** pets

c. Some new **big brothers and sisters** will want to be held the same way the baby is being held.

Some will even want to be breast-fed. If the older sibling is young enough, your partner may actually want to give in to the request. If so, it should be on a very temporary basis.

TIP Giving a couple of teaspoons of breast milk might be a better solution; most older kids won't like the watery consistency or the sweet taste.

Staying at home with a newborn is a thankless task. Your partner needs to know that you _____ what she's doing.

    **a.** approve of
    **b.** are jealous of
    **c.** wouldn't do
    **d.** appreciate

# A

d.  Staying at home with a newborn is a thankless task. Your partner needs to know that you **appreciate** what she's doing.

You barely get any adult time together, and neither of you is getting your needs met. Add sleep deprivation and a few dis-agreements on parenting, and you've got a recipe for conflict.

TIP Buy her flowers, go out on dates, take the baby (even if it's only for a half hour), and let your partner take a break. Don't be surprised if all she wants to do is shower and take a nap.

MONTHS

Although most of your baby's vocalizing is _____ , he's making some delightful single-syllable sounds.

    **a.** random
    **b.** obnoxious
    **c.** crying
    **d.** out of tune

c. Although most of your baby's vocalizing is **crying**, he's making some delightful single-syllable sounds.

He's now also attentively listening to all the sounds around him and distinguishes speech from any other sound.

TIP If you listen carefully, you should be able to tell the difference between his "Feed me now," "Put me down, I want to take a nap," and "Change my diaper" cries. Those cries are baby-specific, so you won't have much luck deciphering anyone else's baby's "language."

Although _____ of all SIDS babies have no risk factors, there are still a few things you and your partner can do.

    **a.** half
    **b.** two-thirds
    **c.** one-tenth
    **d.** 90%

b. Although **two-thirds** of all SIDS babies have no risk factors, there are still a few things you and your partner can do.

Your worries about SIDS are perfectly reasonable. But put them into perspective: As frightening as it is, 1,999 out of every 2,000 babies don't die of it.

TIP To reduce your baby's SIDS risk, make sure your baby sleeps on her back on a firm mattress, don't smoke (and don't let anyone else smoke near the baby), don't overdress the baby, and have your partner breastfeed the baby.

When we face an immense emotional upheaval, such as ____ , too many of us have no idea how to react.

    **a.** missing a meal
    **b.** a new baby
    **c.** the loss of a child
    **d.** changing a job

c. When we face an immense emotional upheaval, such as **the loss of a child**, too many of us have no idea how to react.

Losing a child is something no one who hasn't experienced it can possibly imagine. The toll can be physical, emotional, and psychological.

TIP Couples who've experienced this kind of tragedy stayed together by communicating with each other, acknowledging that men and women grieve differently, and agreeing not to blame each other.

You may find yourself spending
a lot of time thinking about your
\_\_\_\_\_ .

    **a.** senior prom
    **b.** education
    **c.** new baby
    **d.** own father

# A

d. You may find yourself spending a lot of time thinking about your **own father**.

Was he the kind of dad you'd like to use as a role model, or was he exactly the kind of father you don't want to be? Was he supportive and nurturing, or was he just the opposite? If your father was absent or abusive you may worry that you'll do the same, and you may emotionally and/or physically pull back from your baby as a way of protecting him from you.

Adopted children and their adoptive fathers _____ in very much the same ways as biologically related fathers and kids.

    **a.** play poker
    **b.** learn
    **c.** develop
    **d.** love

# A

c. Adopted children and their adoptive fathers **develop** in very much the same ways as biologically related fathers and kids.

Many feel inadequate at not having been able to produce their own children, although within a few years, most have come to terms with not having a biological child.

TIP If you're having trouble accepting that you won't be having biologically related children, talk to some other people about what you're feeling. Start with your partner.

With more and more women in the workforce, there's a lot of pressure on new moms to _____ .

**a.** stay home
**b.** go back to school
**c.** start a business
**d.** go back to work

d. With more and more women in the workforce, there's a lot of pressure on new moms to **go back to work**.

That explains why a third of them are on the job again only 6 weeks after giving birth, and two-thirds are working after 12 weeks.

TIP This can be a very tough time for your partner, and she's going to need your help and support to get through it.

# 3 MONTHS

Introduce your baby to _____ now if you haven't done so already.

    **a.** spicy Thai food
    **b.** your friends
    **c.** a bottle
    **d.** time travel

A

c. Introduce your baby to **a bottle** now if you haven't done so already.

If you wait too long, you may miss your window of opportunity. Some babies may get used to the feel of a silicone nipple but others will refuse. Having breast milk in the bottles will up your chances that the baby will take them.

───

TIP Ideally, you should give the baby the bottle. Babies have a keen sense of smell. If the baby smells mom but gets something other than a breast in her mouth, she could get confused.

Deciding to be a stay-at-home dad is a decision that will _____ your family.

    **a.** affect everyone in
    **b.** horrify
    **c.** ruin
    **d.** thrill

a. Deciding to be a stay-at-home dad is a decision that will **affect everyone in** your family.

More men are discovering the joys of being an at-home dad. If nothing else, you won't have to worry about day care, you'll build a strong relationship with your child, and it'll do great things for your partner's career.

———

TIP Ask yourself these questions: Can we afford it? Can I take the career hit? Can I handle it? Can our relationship handle it?

_____ with your baby is one of the most important things you can do for him.

    **a.** Flying
    **b.** Playing
    **c.** Scuba diving
    **d.** Watching TV

A

b. **Playing** with your baby is one of the most important things you can do for him.

Early parent-child play speeds up the attachment process. Also, babies who play a lot—especially with Dad—are more attentive and interactive and have higher self-esteem than kids who don't get as much physical activity.

TIP Before you mount that basketball hoop, keep in mind that babies at this age have only just discovered themselves. Watching and experimenting with their own little bodies is quite enough to keep them occupied.

# 3 MONTHS

_____

Early this month your baby will
probably tentatively reach for
_____ objects with both hands at
the same time.

    **a.** sharp objects
    **b.** the cat
    **c.** interesting-looking
    **d.** the future

A

c. Early this month your baby will probably tentatively reach for **interesting-looking** objects with both hands at the same time.

Within a few weeks, though, she'll start using her hands independently.

TIP Whether she's using one hand or two, just make sure that whatever you give her is soft enough that she can smack herself in the head without doing any damage—she's going to be doing that a lot.

Babies come prewired for _____ .

    **a.** math
    **b.** hunger
    **c.** emotional manipulation
    **d.** music

A

d. One of the great **myths about** babies is that you have to bundle them up like Nanook of the North.

Here's the truth: overdressed babies are at risk of getting heat stroke, which can result in abnormally high fevers and even convulsions. This risk is especially high if you're taking the baby out in a sling, backpack, or frontpack, where she'll be even hotter.

TIP Dress your baby just as you would dress yourself (except you won't be wearing those cute little booties) plus one layer.

For the first six months, your baby should be kept far away from _____ .

    **a.** direct sunlight
    **b.** reality TV
    **c.** grandparents
    **d.** breast milk

A

a. For the first six months, your baby should be kept far away from **direct sunlight**.

Because babies' skin is at its thinnest and lightest now, even a little sun can do a lot of damage. This applies to babies of all races and skin tones.

TIP When you go out, dress your baby in lightweight and light-colored, long-sleeved shirts and long pants. Try to stay out of the sun between 10 a.m. and 2 p.m. If you absolutely must go out in the sun, make sure the baby is wearing a wide-brimmed hat.

---

Until he's _____ old, don't use
any sunscreen on your baby at
all.

    **a.** 2 years
    **b.** six months
    **c.** very, very
    **d.** 5 years

A

---

b. Until he's **six months** old, don't use any sunscreen on your baby at all.

Most sunscreens are filled with chemicals and frequently cause allergic reactions.

---

TIP After six months, the risk of an allergic reaction from sunscreen is much lower, but stick with one that's unscented, alcohol- and PABA-free, and hypoallergenic, or made specially for infants.

No matter what you do or how hard you try, one of these days your baby is going to get _____ .

    **a.** diaper rash
    **b.** angry
    **c.** arrested
    **d.** all grown up

a. No matter what you do or how hard you try, one of these days your baby is going to get **diaper rash**.

It's almost impossible to completely prevent diaper rash. When it develops, let your baby frolic for a few minutes sans diaper. The extra air circulation will help.

TIP To keep diaper rash to a minimum, change your baby's diapers even if they're only slightly wet. As a preventive measure, apply some diaper cream to the baby's bottom with each change.

MONTHS

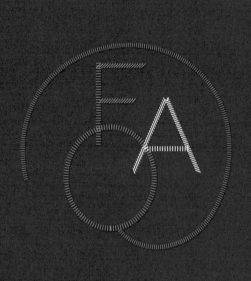

Your baby can now track moving objects, coordinating the activities of her eyes and head as well as _____ .

    **a.** an adult can
    **b.** her hands
    **c.** crawl
    **d.** a hungry wolf cub

b. Your baby now knows that **his hands and feet** are extensions of himself.

He'll spend a great deal of time every day staring at his hands and using them to explore his face, his mouth, and whatever other parts of his body he can reach. He's also learning that objects have labels and may occasionally respond to his own name.

She's trying as hard as she can to _____ , using her tongue and changing the shape of her mouth.

    **a.** spit
    **b.** whistle
    **c.** speak
    **d.** sing

A

c. She's trying as hard as she can to **speak**, using her tongue and changing the shape of her mouth.

If she's got something on her mind, she may take the initiative and start a "conversation" with you. If she really wants to chat, she'll be very upset if you aren't focusing all your attention on her.

More than _____ working dads say they experience work/family conflict.

   **a.** 70% of
   **b.** a dozen
   **c.** 10% of
   **d.** 40% of

a. More than **70% of** working dads say they experience work/family conflict.

And in recent studies, 80% or more of men aged 20 to 39 said that having a work schedule that allows them to spend time with their family is more important than doing challenging work or earning a high salary.

Before their babies are born, nearly all expectant fathers feel that \_\_\_\_\_ is the best way to feed a baby.

    **a.** solid food
    **b.** breast-feeding
    **c.** formula
    **d.** letting mom do it

b. Before their babies are born, nearly all expectant fathers feel that **breast-feeding** is the best way to feed a baby.

After the baby comes, new fathers still feel that breast is best, but they may also feel a little ambivalent. Many admit to feeling that nothing they do to satisfy their child can ever compete with their partner's breasts.

TIP Many dads also feel a sense of relief when their partner weans the baby and gives him the opportunity to "catch up."

Becoming a father makes some men wonder whether they've retained _____ .

    **a.** MacGyver
    **b.** Chuck Norris
    **c.** your father
    **d.** their masculinity

d. Becoming a father makes some men wonder whether they've retained **their masculinity**.

Too often, dads "solve" this problem by leaving all the child-rearing to their partner.

TIP Your choice: Accept the hardest yet most rewarding challenge you'll probably ever face by becoming an actively involved father and taking on a significant share of the responsibility for raising your children, or take the easy way out and leave it all to someone else. What would a *real* man do?

Children are born with a set of
9 fundamental traits called
"_____."

   **a.** temperament
   **b.** quirks
   **c.** Tempur-Pedic
   **d.** hierarchy of needs

a. Children are born with a set of 9 fundamental traits called "**temperament.**"

These qualities, which experts now believe remain fairly consistent throughout life, combine differently for each child and determine, to a great extent, a child's personality and whether he will be "easy" or "challenging."

Some babies just make a lot of noise, and short of leaving the room or \_\_\_\_\_ , there's not much you can do.

    **a.** cranking up the volume
    **b.** yelling back
    **c.** ignoring it
    **d.** getting earplugs

A

d. Some babies just make a lot of noise, and short of leaving the room or **getting earplugs**, there's not much you can do.

Just make sure you can tell the difference between a shrill, eardrum-destroying "I'm happy" shriek and a shrill, eardrum-destroying "I'm unhappy" one.

TIP Watch out if you're tickling your baby with your nose—her mouth is very, very close to your ears.

168

Not much can make you _____ than going out with a smiling, happy baby.

**a.** prouder and more confident
**b.** feel more important
**c.** look sexier
**d.** smarter

A

a. Not much can make you prouder and more confident than going out with a smiling, happy baby.

But a baby who isn't a smiler, and who whimpers and cries all the time, can be a real challenge to your self-confidence. It's hard to take pleasure in—or even feel proud of—a baby who always seems to be in a bad mood.

TIP The truth is that the lack of a smile probably doesn't mean anything at all. And the whining will subside as your baby's verbal skills improve.

If your baby is really, really active, you might want to put some rubber stops underneath the
_____ .

    **a.** baby
    **b.** crib's wheels
    **c.** kitchen table
    **d.** cat

b. If your baby is really, really active, you might want to put some rubber stops underneath the **crib's wheels**.

Believe me, it's quite a shock to walk into your baby's room first thing in the morning and find that he—and his bed—aren't where you left them.

TIP Your high-activity baby may sometimes be too busy to be held or cuddled, and may squirm and cry until you put him down. It's easy to take this as a rejection, but don't.

If you schedule meals at the same times every day, you may be able to help your unpredictable baby create a _____ .

    **a.** balanced diet
    **b.** solid foundation
    **c.** modified routine
    **d.** new world order

c. If you schedule meals at the same times every day, you may be able to help your unpredictable baby create a **modified routine**.

Routines are important for bedtime, too. If your baby's sleep irregularities are truly serious, you and your partner should divide up the night, each taking a shift while the other sleeps.

TIP If that doesn't help, talk with your pediatrician about baby-relaxation techniques. He or she may also prescribe a mild sedative—for the baby, not you.

For the first few _____ of a highly sensitive baby's life, you'll never know what's going to set her off.

    **a.** days
    **b.** years
    **c.** hours
    **d.** months

d. For the first few **months** of a highly sensitive baby's life, you'll never know what's going to set her off.

One way to make your baby's life a little less jarring is to modify the amount and type of stimulation in her environment.

TIP Avoid neon colors when decorating her room, get opaque drapes to keep daytime light out during naptime, and don't play actively with her right before bedtime.

Your highly distractible/low-persistence baby gets bored easily and may want constant _____ from you.

    **a.** attention
    **b.** cash
    **c.** freedom
    **d.** reassurance

a. Your highly distractible/low-persistence baby gets bored easily and may want constant **attention** from you.

He may also take forever to eat, stopping every 30 seconds to follow a fly as it zips through the room or to check out a shadow on the wall. If he's being breast-fed, this will probably bother your partner more than it does you.

On average, couples resume having sex about _____ after the birth of the baby.

- **a.** 2 years
- **b.** 7 weeks
- **c.** 14 minutes
- **d.** one month

A

b. On average, couples resume having sex about **7 weeks** after the birth of the baby.

But be aware: It could be a lot longer than that before your pre-baby and pre-pregnancy sex life returns.

TIP To jump-start your sex life, try going for quality over quantity and do everything you can to spice things up: watch some porn videos (together, of course), make out in the back-seat of the car (you may have to remove the baby's car seat), or send each other a few sexts during the day.

At all costs, do *not* become your baby's _____ .

   **a.** sugar daddy
   **b.** chauffeur
   **c.** sleep-transition object
   **d.** banker

A

c. At all costs, do *not* become your baby's **sleep-transition object**.

Your baby's last waking memory should be of her crib or something familiar (like a toy, a picture on the wall, or the glow-in-the-dark stars you stuck to the ceiling). That way, if she wakes up in the middle of the night, she'll see the familiar object and associate it with sleep.

TIP If you were the last thing she sees before dropping off, when she wakes up she'll want you again—even if you happen to be sleeping.

Sometimes, no matter what you do, your baby is going to wake up \_\_\_\_ .

    **a.** singing
    **b.** angry
    **c.** at 2 or 3 a.m.
    **d.** in another part of the house

c. Sometimes, no matter what you do, your baby is going to wake up **at 2 or 3 a.m.**

When this happens, keep your middle-of-the-night encounters as boring as possible. Until they're old enough to be having sex, kids need to know that nighttime is for sleeping.

MONTHS

This month's big discovery is, yes, _____ .

**a.** toes
**b.** fire
**c.** ears
**d.** shale oil

# A

a. This month's big discovery
is, yes, **toes**.

Just as your baby used to spend
hours fondling and sucking
his own fingers, he'll repeat
the process with his lower
extremities.

Your baby can get himself from her tummy to _____ .

**a.** airborne
**b.** standing position
**c.** a handstand
**d.** her hands and knees

d. Your baby can get himself from his tummy to **her hands and knees**.

Once she's there, she's not quite sure what to do, so she may rock back and forth as if anxious for some kind of race to begin.

It's finally happened: your baby
is _____ .

    **a.** talking
    **b.** walking
    **c.** babbling
    **d.** doing calculus

c. It's finally happened: your baby is **babbling**.

He's so delighted with his new-found language skills that he'll babble for 20 to 30 minutes at a stretch.

TIP Don't worry if you're not there to enjoy it—he's perfectly content to talk to his toys or, in a pinch, to himself.

She's capable of _____ a growing number of emotions: fear,
anger, disgust, and satisfaction.

    **a.** recognizing
    **b.** describing
    **c.** mimicking
    **d.** expressing

d. She's capable of **expressing** a growing number of emotions: fear, anger, disgust, and satisfaction.

Your baby knows the difference between familiar people and strangers, and associates friends with pleasure. Unfortunately, she doesn't remember that her friends started off as strangers. Consequently, she's a little slow to warm to new people.

---

TIP That can be tough on you if you're trying to show people what a fantastic baby you have, but it's a positive developmental sign.

Many women have been raised to believe that if they aren't _____ , they've failed as mothers.

   **a.** pregnant
   **b.** earning more money than you
   **c.** the primary caregiver
   **d.** breast-feeding

c. Many women have been raised to believe that if they aren't **the primary caregiver**, they've failed as mothers.

In some cases, this leads the mom to act as a "gatekeeper," not sharing the parenting, and actually limiting the dad's involvement to an amount she feels isn't a threat.

———

TIP If you're feeling left out, talk to your partner immediately. Chances are she's not doing it deliberately. Show her that you're serious about being an equal participant.

By six months after their children's birth, about 95% of new fathers are back _____ .

  **a.** to their prebirth weight
  **b.** working full-time
  **c.** watching sports
  **d.** with an old girlfriend

A

b. By six months after their children's birth, about 95% of new fathers are back **working full-time**.

As it turns out, men are at least as likely as women to suffer from work-family spillover—family pressures intruding on work, and work pressures intruding on family life. Working moms and dads are also equally likely to say that trying to manage the spillover causes them a lot of stress.

There are a few ways you can maximize your time with your family, minimize your stress, and avoid _____ your career.

    **a.** advancing
    **b.** stalling
    **c.** trashing
    **d.** fast-tracking

c. There are a few ways you can maximize your time with your family, minimize your stress, and avoid **trashing** your career.

According to the Society for Human Resource Management, 60% of companies offer some kind of flexible work arrangement (FWA), including compressed workweeks, at least some telecommuting, flextime, and job sharing.

———

TIP Talk to your HR department about the FWAs they may have. Some companies don't always tell everyone about them.

---

If you can't (or don't want to) reduce your _____ , you may still be able to build a little flexibility into your schedule.

- **a.** weight
- **b.** workload
- **c.** salary
- **d.** hours

d.  If you can't (or don't want to) reduce your **hours**, you may still be able to build a little flexibility into your schedule.

Options to explore include flextime, a compressed workweek (such as four 10-hour days), or working an alternative workweek (such as Wednesday–Sunday instead of Monday–Friday).

Most companies still look at flexible or alternative workplace schedules as a " _____ ."

    **a.** net loss
    **b.** pipe dream
    **c.** women's issue
    **d.** unicorn

c. Most companies still look at flexible or alternative workplace schedules as a "women's issue."

If you're an employer or supervisor, the ultimate responsibility for changing this Neanderthal attitude and helping men get more involved with their families rests at the top—with you.

TIP Companies with family-friendly policies find that the costs are more than offset by increased morale and productivity, reduced absenteeism, and lower turnover, all of which have bottom-line impact.

No matter how you try to keep your work life separate from your family life, there's going to be plenty of _____ .

**a.** spillover
**b.** beers left
**c.** free time
**d.** fun

a. No matter how you try to keep your work life separate from your family life, there's going to be plenty of **spillover**.

This isn't necessarily a bad thing. Fatherhood researcher John Snarey found that, "contrary to the stereotype of rigid work-family trade-off, a positive, reciprocal interaction may exist between childrearing and breadwinning." In other words, skills you've honed at work may make you a better dad and being a dad may make you a better employee.

Integrating old and new families can be enormously _____ for your kids, your new partner, and you.

    **a.** entertaining
    **b.** complicated
    **c.** expensive
    **d.** frustrating

A

b. Integrating old and new families can be enormously **complicated** for your kids, your new partner, and you.

But whatever you do, don't give in to pressure or temptation to sever ties with your older children. They need you, and you need them, even if you don't get to see each other as often as you'd like.

TIP Your challenge is to create a new family unit, one that integrates your older children, your new child, and your partner.

---

Older siblings aren't the only children who get _____ .

    **a.** gas
    **b.** chores
    **c.** jealous
    **d.** an allowance

c. Older siblings aren't the only children who get jealous.

British researcher Riccardo Draghi-Lorenz asked 24 mothers of five-month-old babies to show affection to another baby and to talk with another adult while their baby watched. Over half of the babies got upset and cried when Mom cooed, tickled, or cuddled with another infant.

Even if you're tempted to start solids earlier than six months,

_____ .

    **a.** resist the urge
    **b.** go with it
    **c.** start with beef jerky
    **d.** go organic

# A

a. Even if you're tempted to start solids earlier than six months, **resist the urge**.

Because younger babies' digestive systems are immature, they can't digest proteins, starches, or fats until they're at least six months old. In addition, breastfeeding for longer has been shown to strengthen the baby's immune system and protect against a variety of illnesses.

TIP If you start introducing solids before your baby is physically able to chew and swallow, you run the risk that he could choke on something.

If your baby was born prematurely, check with your pediatrician before _____ .

    **a.** base jumping
    **b.** introducing solids
    **c.** panic sets in
    **d.** breast-feeding

A

b. If your baby was born prematurely, check with your pediatrician before **introducing solids**.

You'll still probably start when her adjusted age is six months. (If she's five months old now and was born 6 weeks early, her adjusted age, for food introduction purposes, is only three and a half months.)

Fewer than _____ of children under 3 are truly allergic to any foods.

   **a.** 8%
   **b.** 20%
   **c.** 1%
   **d.** 5%

# A

d. Fewer than 5% of children under 3 are truly allergic to any foods.

Fortunately, most kids—except those allergic to peanuts and fish—outgrow their allergies by age 5. (Only 2% of children over 5 have true food allergies.)

TIP Introduce one food at a time, watching carefully for reactions, and waiting a few days before introducing another food. That way, if your baby has a reaction, you'll immediately know what caused it.

When your baby is ready to feed himself, he'll let you know, usually by grabbing the ____ from your hand.

    **a.** spoon
    **b.** phone
    **c.** coffee
    **d.** check

a. When your baby is ready to feed himself, he'll let you know, usually by grabbing the **spoon** from your hand.

When this happens, prepare yourself. Over the course of the next few weeks, your baby will discover the joys of sticking various kinds of food in his nose and eyes, under his chin, behind his ears, and in his hair. And it won't be much longer until he learns to throw.

MONTHS

By the end of this month your baby will probably be able to sit by herself in _____ position.

    **a.** tripod
    **b.** lotus
    **c.** tailor
    **d.** an awkward

a. By the end of this month your baby will probably be able to sit by herself in **tripod** position.

She may even be able to right herself if she tips over, and pull herself to a sitting position if you grasp her hands. She can now look at one thing and reach for another, and can probably pass objects back and forth between her hands.

Your baby recognizes _____ and, if he's not too busy, may turn his head toward you if you call him.

    **a.** weather patterns
    **b.** his name
    **c.** your partner's perfume
    **d.** the caller ID

# A

b. Your baby recognizes **his name** and, if he's not too busy, may turn his head toward you if you call him.

With so many new things to do and learn, your baby is now awake about 12 hours a day and spends most of that time finding out about his environment by touching, holding, tasting, and shaking things. He'll also get confused if he sees a picture of you but hears someone else's voice.

She's getting pretty good at imitating sounds and also tries—with some success—to imitate your _____ .

    **a.** voice
    **b.** walk
    **c.** inflections
    **d.** posture

c. She's getting pretty good at imitating sounds and also tries—with some success—to imitate your **inflections**.

She's getting so familiar with language that she can easily tell the difference between conversational speech and any of the other noises you make. She might, for example, laugh when you start making animal noises. And she definitely prefers listening to her native language over a foreign one.

# 6 MONTHS

Until this month, your baby really didn't care who fed him, changed him, or hugged him, just as long as _____ .

    **a.** it was mom
    **b.** it wasn't you
    **c.** it was free
    **d.** it got done

## A

d. Until this month, your baby really didn't care who fed him, changed him, or hugged him, just as long as it got done.

For about 50–80% of babies, *who* satisfies their needs is almost as important. You, your partner, and perhaps a few other very familiar people may now be the only ones your baby will allow near him without crying.

TIP This is the beginning of stranger anxiety.

The single emotion that can be the most destructive and disruptive to your experience of fatherhood is _____ .

   **a.** love
   **b.** hate
   **c.** jealousy
   **d.** tenderness

c. The single emotion that can be the most destructive and disruptive to your experience of fatherhood is **jealousy.**

As with most emotions, a little jealousy goes a long way. Too much can make you feel competitive toward or resentful of your partner, the babysitter, or even the baby.

TIP You'll be surprised at how common jealousy is. But watch out: Its "potential for destruction lies not in having the feelings but in burying them," writes Dr. Martin Greenberg.

Things that would have had you
panicking a few months ago
now seem _____ .

   **a.** completely ordinary
   **b.** way worse than you'd
      imagined
   **c.** laughable
   **d.** totally foreign

A

a. Things that would have had you panicking a few months ago now seem completely ordinary.

You probably feel more connected and attached to your baby than ever before. The calmness and smoothness of this period can (but don't always) spill over into your marriage as well.

TIP This is a time when a lot of men say that their relationship with their partner has gotten "easier." You may finally have a sense of truly being a family.

---

There are _____ things you can do to reinforce cause-and-effect thinking.

   **a.** very few
   **b.** 7
   **c.** a handful of
   **d.** thousands of

d. There are **thousands of** things you can do to reinforce cause-and-effect thinking.

Rattles, banging games, rolling a ball back and forth, and splashing in the pool are excellent. Baby gyms—especially the kind that make a lot of noise when smacked—are also good.

---

TIP Be sure to pack up the baby gym the moment your baby starts trying to pull herself up on it; most gyms aren't sturdy enough to support much weight.

The important idea that _____ can exist even when they're out of sight is finally sinking in.

    **a.** objects
    **b.** babies
    **c.** cupcakes
    **d.** oxygen

# A

a. The important idea that **objects** can exist even when they're out of sight is finally sinking in.

This is what *object permanence* is all about, and it develops in stages.

TIP Peekaboo and other games that involve hiding and finding things are great for developing object permanence. Peekaboo in particular teaches your baby an excellent lesson: When you go away, you always come back.

Starting at this age, babies will anticipate where _____ are going to land.

    **a.** fly balls
    **b.** dropped objects
    **c.** space shuttles
    **d.** birds

# A

b. Starting at this age, babies will anticipate where **dropped objects** are going to land.

Put your baby in a high chair and sit down at a table facing her. Slowly move a toy horizontally in front of her a few times. Then put a cereal box between you and the baby, and move the ball along the same trajectory but have it go behind the box for a second or two. Most six-month-olds will look ahead to the other side of the box, anticipating where the ball will emerge.

When searching for in-home caregivers, the first thing to do is to conduct _____ over the phone.

    **a.** cold calls
    **b.** orchestras
    **c.** thorough interviews
    **d.** a stand-up routine

A

c. When searching for in-home caregivers, the first thing to do is to conduct **thorough interviews** over the phone.

This will enable you to screen out the obviously unacceptable candidates, like those looking only for a month-long job or the ones without a license if you need someone who can drive.

TIP Invite the candidates who make the first cut over to meet you and your partner in person. Be sure they come at a time when the baby is awake so you can watch each one in action.

---

Having an au pair can be a wonderful opportunity for you and your baby to learn about _____ .

    **a.** another culture
    **b.** teen issues
    **c.** indentured servitude
    **d.** infidelity

A

a. Having an au pair can be a wonderful opportunity for you and your baby to learn about **another culture**.

In theory, an au pair is supposed to do a lot of childcare, perhaps some light baby-related house-keeping, and take 6 semester hours of academic credit. But in reality she may be far more interested in going to the mall with her new American friends or hanging out with your neighbor's teenage son.

---

TIP An au pair is not a house-keeper, nurse, or professionally trained childcare worker.

If you hire an in-home care-giver, you'll need to get a _____ .

  **a.** limo
  **b.** federal tax ID number
  **c.** second job
  **d.** complete physical exam

b. If you hire an in-home caregiver, you'll need to get a **federal tax ID number**.

You may also need to register with your state tax department, calculate payroll deductions (and, of course, deduct them), file quarterly reports with the IRS and your state tax board, and more.

In commercial day-care facilities, there should be a good balance of playtime, story time, and _____ .

    **a.** unsupervised time
    **b.** more playtime
    **c.** naptime
    **d.** Texas Hold'em

A

c. In commercial day-care facilities, there should be a good balance of playtime, story time, and **naptime**.

Other things to consider: Is the atmosphere bright and pleasant? Is there a fenced-in outdoor play area with a variety of safe equipment? Can the caregivers see the entire playground at all times? Are there different areas for resting, quiet play, and active play? Are there enough toys and learning materials for the number of children? Are the toys clean, safe, and within reach of the children?

---

At any day-care facility, ask what precautions they take to make sure kids are picked up only by _____ .

    **a.** you
    **b.** FedEx
    **c.** a limo driver
    **d.** people you select

A

d. At any day-care facility, ask what precautions they take to make sure kids are picked up only by **people you select**.

There are a lot of sick people out there and you don't want one of them strolling into the daycare center and walking out with your baby.

Finding a good childcare provider is a lengthy and involved process. Don't give up until you're completely _____ .

    **a.** exhausted
    **b.** satisfied
    **c.** defeated
    **d.** bored

b. Finding a good childcare provider is a lengthy and involved process. Don't give up until you're completely **satisfied**.

Unfortunately, most parents get frustrated with the choices and end up settling for something less than optimal. The result? A recent study found that only 8% of childcare facilities were considered "good quality," and 40% were rated "less than minimal." Worst of all, 10–20% of children "get care so poor that it risks damaging their development." So be careful.

MONTHS

Your baby can now get himself to a sitting position from his

_____ .

**a.** back
**b.** side
**c.** stomach
**d.** feet

A

c. Your baby can now get himself to a sitting position from his **stomach**.

Your baby is learning to change his position and can move through several positions with ease.

———

TIP Encourage him as he learns to put himself in different positions. Assist him at first, then sit back and watch with pride as he learns to do it himself.

Sometimes your baby will _____ instead of crawl.

    **a.** roll around
    **b.** scoot on her butt
    **c.** flop on her belly
    **d.** walk

b. Sometimes your baby will **scoot on her butt** instead of crawl.

Not all babies crawl in the traditional hands-and-knees way. Some prefer to scoot around on their butt, using one arm to pull and the other to push. Some use a hybrid method: one foot flat on the floor as if trying to stand, and one knee on the floor in regular crawling position.

If you hold your baby _____ , she'll put weight on her feet, stomp, and bounce up and down.

    **a.** upright
    **b.** on her belly
    **c.** on her back
    **d.** upside down

# A

a. If you hold your baby **upright**, she'll put weight on her feet, stomp, and bounce up and down.

This is one of those fascinating reflexes. Of course she's nowhere near able to walk, but she's getting in a little practice bearing her own weight and controlling her feet.

TIP As her legs get stronger and she can control them better, gradually allow her to bear more and more of her own weight. This will help her develop her leg muscles, which she'll be using a lot of soon.

If your partner is still breast-feeding, you might start to hear a few yelps from her during feeding time, as the baby is now
_____ .

    **a.** talking too much
    **b.** blowing bubbles
    **c.** nursing less
    **d.** using his teeth

# A

d.  If your partner is still breast-feeding, you might start to hear a few yelps from her during feeding time, as the baby is now **using his teeth**.

Baby teeth are sharp, and if your partner is still nursing, she feels every edge every time she feeds him.

---

TIP Be supportive and compassionate. Breast-feeding may no longer be the pleasant bonding moment it was just a few months ago.

Your baby is learning to _____ items that are similar but different.

    **a.** compare
    **b.** organize
    **c.** separate
    **d.** sell

A

a. Your baby is learning to **compare** items that are similar but different.

If you give your baby several blocks that are similar but not identical, she'll look at each one closely, manipulate it, and line them up for comparison.

TIP Give her plenty of opportunity to practice these skills by having a variety of blocks, balls, or toys that are different sizes or colors.

When it comes to your baby's vocabulary, she's forgetting how to _____ that aren't part of her native language.

    **a.** make sounds
    **b.** cook traditional foods
    **c.** use swear words
    **d.** make animal noises

# A

a. When it comes to your baby's vocabulary, she's forgetting how to **make sounds** that aren't part of her native language.

Your baby used to be able to produce any sound a human can make. But since she now spends all of her time trying to repeat the sounds you make, she's forgetting how to make the ones you don't use, such as rolled *r*'s or the clicks of some indigenous peoples.

Your baby's babbling is shifting to _____ .

    **a.** humorous impressions
    **b.** monotone sounds
    **c.** operatic singing
    **d.** multisyllable words

# A

d. Your baby's babbling is shifting to **multisyllable** words.

The "ba-ba, ma-ma, da-da" vocabulary you're used to hearing from your sweet baby is being replaced by "babababa, mamamama, dadadada." He modulates the tone, volume, and speed of his sounds and actively tries to communicate with you.

---

TIP Your baby now tries to get in a few "words" after you speak, and he may wait for you to finish your thought before "responding." Have fun with this first step toward great communication.

Although she's fascinated by objects, your baby really prefers _____ .

    **a.** playing chess
    **b.** watching television
    **c.** reading a book
    **d.** social interactions

# A

d. Although she's fascinated by objects, your baby really prefers **social interactions**.

Your baby loves to pick up, stare at, and manipulate objects. But she really loves communicating with other humans (although, in a pinch, she'll try to chat up your pet or one of her stuffed animals).

TIP One-on-one activities like reading, chasing, and fetching are great ways to interact with your baby and strengthen your relationship.

Your baby can now tell the difference between _____ .

    **a.** primary colors
    **b.** dogs and cats
    **c.** adults and children
    **d.** television characters

c. Your baby can now tell the difference between **adults and children.**

In the same way that dogs are instinctively drawn to other dogs, your baby may be becoming especially interested in playing alongside kids his own age.

———

TIP Create as many opportunities as you can for your baby to interact with other children. Although he's not ready to play *with* them, he'll still enjoy the company as he plays *next* to them.

Your baby has learned to recognize and react differently to _____ .

    **a.** reward and punishment
    **b.** positive and negative tones
    **c.** tears and laughter
    **d.** dogs barking

A

b. Your baby has learned to recognize and react differently to **positive and negative tones**.

The way you respond to your baby has a big influence on her behavior. In other words, *how* you say something is often more important than what you're actually saying.

TIP If you seem angry or frightened by something she's done, she may cry because she knows she upset you. But your smile and encouraging words could be enough to soothe her tears or overcome her fears.

Strangers may continue to make your baby _____ .

    **a.** shy and anxious
    **b.** laugh
    **c.** angry
    **d.** uncomfortable

# A

a. Strangers may continue to make your baby **shy and anxious**.

He may also become fussy or upset if you leave him with one of those strangers.

TIP If you do have to leave your baby with someone he doesn't know very well, be as upbeat and positive as you can. Then, say goodbye and walk away. If you look worried or hang around too long, you're confirming his suspicion that there actually *is* something to worry about. And that will just upset him even more.

As her mission to imitate everything you do continues, your
baby now insists on _____ .

- **a.** changing her own diaper
- **b.** finger-feeding herself
- **c.** texting
- **d.** going potty

# A

---

b. As her mission to imitate everything you do continues, your baby now insists on **finger-feeding herself.**

As your baby moves closer to independence (at least in her own mind), she'll want to do more and more on her own. Feeding herself is just the beginning.

---

TIP Because just about everything she picks up still goes in his mouth—whether it's edible or not—make sure to keep small objects well out of reach. At the same time, give her plenty of opportunities to do things for herself.

The easiest way to find out what your baby is thinking at this age is to teach him _____ .

    **a.** sign language
    **b.** to talk
    **c.** to write
    **d.** to text

# A

a. The easiest way to find out what your baby is thinking at this age is to teach him **sign language.**

Children with hearing-impaired parents who teach them to sign are able to start communicating before nine months of age. Children with 2 hearing parents don't usually have much to say before their first birthday.

TIP There are a number of ways to teach your child (and yourself) to sign. Most are based on American Sign Language. Keep your expectations reasonable and make it fun.

Most dentists agree that sucking on a pacifier is fine until about _____ .

    **a.** 1 year of age
    **b.** 16 years of age
    **c.** 3 years of age
    **d.** 4 years of age

A

d. Most dentists agree that sucking on a pacifier is fine until about 4 **years of age**.

A lot of babies have a need to suck that can't be satisfied by breast-feeding or shoving their own (or your) fingers in their mouth. Most dentists agree that pacifier-sucking isn't a problem until about age 4. Pacifier use may also reduce the risk of sudden infant death syndrome (SIDS).

TIP Never, ever tie a pacifier around the baby's neck or use string to attach it to your baby's clothes. Instead, get a pacifier tether that clips on—and comes off easily.

Most kids have _____ teeth by the end of their first year.

    **a.** 4
    **b.** 6
    **c.** 8
    **d.** 10

c. Most kids have **8** teeth by the end of their first year.

The middle bottom teeth come in first, followed by the 2 middle teeth on top, then the ones on either side. Although some teeth come in without any trouble, most kids experience at least some discomfort for a few days.

TIP If your baby is especially miserable, your pediatrician may recommend some acetaminophen drops. Massaging your baby's gums might help, and teething rings, teething biscuits, frozen bagels, or frozen bananas may offer some relief, too.

If you haven't _____ your home yet, now's the time to start.

    **a.** dusted
    **b.** organized
    **c.** purchased
    **d.** childproofed

d. If you haven't **childproofed** your home yet, now's the time to start.

Now that your baby is mobile, his mission in life is to locate the most dangerous, life-threatening things in your home and scare the hell out of you.

————

TIP Get down on your hands and knees and look at the world from your baby's perspective. Don't those lamp cords and speaker wires look like they'd be fun to yank or chew on? And don't those power outlets look like they'd be fun to stick something in?

Install _____ on your oven and all low cabinets and drawers in your kitchen and bathrooms.

    **a.** handles
    **b.** safety locks
    **c.** keyed locks
    **d.** magnets

b. Install **safety locks** on your oven and all low cabinets and drawers in your kitchen and bathrooms.

For kitchen and bathroom drawers, install locks that allow the doors to be opened a little bit (but not enough to get a hand in), but also keep the drawer or door from closing and smashing tiny fingers. And don't forget about toilet locks. Babies and water are not a good combination.

TIP Choose one kitchen cabinet and leave the lock off. Stock it with unbreakable pots and pans and let your baby go nuts.

After six months, you should use sunblock on your baby any time you're outside, even if it's _____ .

    **a.** cloudy
    **b.** rainy
    **c.** winter
    **d.** nighttime

A

a. After six months, you should use sunblock on your baby any time you're outside, even if it's **cloudy**.

UV rays still get through the clouds and can burn your baby badly—even if it's cool outside.

TIP Water, snow, and sand can all reflect and intensify the sun's light and heat. Be sure to use a high-SPF, waterproof sunblock that protects against UVA and UVB, and reapply it often. Don't skimp on this.

**8 MONTHS**

Although your baby will learn to stand up this month, she'll have difficulty _____ .

    **a.** remaining standing
    **b.** sitting back down
    **c.** making calls on her own
    **d.** getting airborne

b. Although your baby will learn to stand up this month, she'll have difficulty **sitting back down**.

**The ability to stand up and lock the knees in order to stay upright comes more quickly than the ability to unlock those knees and go the other direction.**

# 8 MONTHS

Your baby is now using his _____
to pick up tiny objects.

    **a.** thumb and first finger
    **b.** whole hand
    **c.** toes
    **d.** chopsticks

a. Your baby is now using his **thumb and first finger** to pick up tiny objects.

He uses a pincer grip to pick things up and is increasingly fascinated by the most miniscule items.

———

TIP He's getting more coordinated but he's still a baby, so most things he picks up tend to go directly from hand to mouth. That means you'll have to be extra vigilant. Remember, anything that can go through the tube from a standard roll of toilet paper is a potential choking hazard.

# 8 MONTHS

Your baby is so busy now that she may feel that she _____ .

   **a.** needs a secretary
   **b.** needs more sleep
   **c.** should get a raise
   **d.** doesn't have time for naps

A

d. Your baby is so busy now that she may feel that she doesn't have time for naps.

The lack of sleep—together with the frustration of not being able to do everything she wants to do with her body—may make her cranky.

TIP It's not going to be easy, but do everything you can to make sure she gets plenty of rest.

Your baby will now begin
actively looking for toys that he
has seen you _____ .

    **a.** buy
    **b.** throw away
    **c.** play with
    **d.** hide

A

d. Your baby will now begin actively looking for toys that he has seen you **hide**.

As a result, he's almost mastered the idea that objects exist even when they're out of sight.

———

TIP If he's pretty good at finding items he's seen you hide, secretly take the toy he's looking for from the first place and move it. The first few times you do this, he'll be very confused. But pretty soon, he'll learn to look in more than one place.

Your baby knows what happens when objects drop, and that may make her afraid of _____ .

    **a.** falling down stairs
    **b.** falling when she walks
    **c.** flying
    **d.** breaking something

a. She knows what happens when objects drop, and that may make her afraid **of falling down stairs**.

Now that she's seen many things fall, your baby may worry about what would happen if she were to fall—especially if she's seen something break after a fall.

TIP Expect panic at the top of stairs or on high surfaces. Don't force her to do anything that she finds frightening, just smile and reassure her that you're there and that you'll keep her from danger. If you look worried or scared, she'll act accordingly.

Your baby now understands—
and _____ —when you call her
name.

    **a.** ignores you
    **b.** howls
    **c.** responds
    **d.** throws a tantrum

A

c. Your baby now under-
stands—and **responds**—
when you call her name.

She'll also turn her head in response to other familiar noises,
like a car pulling in the drive-
way, the phone ringing, and the
refrigerator opening.

———

TIP At this stage, she has a lot in
common with a pet. Dogs and
cats will come running when
they hear a sound (like a can
being opened) that they associate with getting a treat.

He recognizes his reflection in a mirror and will _____ .

   **a.** apply makeup
   **b.** cry
   **c.** throw things at himself
   **d.** smile at himself

d. He recognizes his reflection in a mirror and will **smile at himself**.

**He may also make faces in the mirror and laugh at the results.**

---

**TIP** Get out your camera, turn it on, and start shooting.

When your baby wants you to pick her up, she'll _____ and bounce around.

    **a.** cry
    **b.** raise her arms
    **c.** send you a text message
    **d.** come right out and say so

A

b. When your baby wants you to pick her up, she'll **raise her arms** and bounce around.

She's getting closer to using actual words, but she knows that nonverbal communication can be more effective. One especially popular message is "up me," which she'll indicate by raising her arms and squirming. In a few months, she'll actually say the words at the same time.

———

TIP When she raises her arms, pick her up. This shows that you understand and will encourage her to communicate even more.

Many men find that caring for a baby makes them more _____ with other people's feelings and emotions.

**a.** disgusted
**b.** empathetic
**c.** sympathetic
**d.** apathetic

A

a. What you read to your baby is not as important as **how** you read it.

Reading the words is great. But hamming it up will make it much more fun for both of you.

TIP Make up funny voices when reading quotations. Make sound effects to mimic movement on the pages. If the words are rhythmical, say them rhythmically while varying your tone. Or sing them, even if you can't carry a tune. Don't worry, your baby's an infant, not a music critic.

Many women believe that the way their children _____ reflects on their abilities as mothers.

    **a.** fill their diapers
    **b.** attract attention
    **c.** dance
    **d.** are dressed

d. Many women believe that the way their children **are dressed** reflects on their abilities as mothers.

Unfortunately, they're probably right.

———

TIP Guys tend to be a lot less worried about how their kids look. Does it really matter if your baby goes out of the house with one blue sock and one red one? When you're taking the baby out yourself, apply your own standards. But if you're going out with your partner, let her pick the baby's wardrobe.

**9 MONTHS**

This month instead of trying to learn new skills, your baby will be _____ old ones.

    **a.** forgetting
    **b.** perfecting
    **c.** recovering from
    **d.** expanding on

A

d. Your baby may now be able to make it **up a flight of stairs** on his own.

But you'd never let your baby crawl **alone on stairs, right?**

If you have stairs in your home, make sure you have secure, impossible-to-pull-down gates at the top and bottom of every staircase.

Your baby can now stand for a few seconds _____ .

   **a.** while eating ice cream
   **b.** all by herself
   **c.** when you're reading to her
   **d.** while holding your hand

d. Your baby can now stand for a few seconds **while holding your hand**.

Your baby's balance is getting better. When sitting, she can turn her body all the way around without falling over. And she can also pull herself up to a standing position and can stay there as long as she's got something to lean on or grab ahold of.

Your baby is now coordinated enough to ____ of 2 or 3 blocks.

    **a.** make a line
    **b.** make a pile
    **c.** build a tower
    **d.** find a basket

A

c. Your baby is now coordinated enough to **build a tower** of 2 or 3 blocks.

Your baby is honing his fine motor skills and he'll spend a lot of time stacking blocks—and then immediately knocking those little towers down.

TIP Always make sure he has plenty of blocks to play with. The more blocks he has, the taller the towers he'll build (and destroy).

Your baby understands that
_____ have consequences.

    **a.** waking you up in the
       middle of the night will
    **b.** swear words
    **c.** crimes
    **d.** actions

d. Your baby understands that **actions** have consequences.

She now fully grasps action/re-action. For example, if she sees you putting on your coat, she knows you're going outside. If you get the stroller too, she'll get excited, knowing she's coming with you. But if you don't take her, she may cry.

He's now getting quite good at expressing _____ .

a. his love
b. preferences
c. hunger
d. packages

A

b. He's now getting quite good at expressing **preferences**.

He can now get you to understand what he wants, by squealing, pointing, grunting, and bouncing. And he'll show you exactly what he doesn't want, too, pushing away things (and people) he has no immediate use for.

Your feelings of connection to your baby will deepen as she becomes more _____ .

    **a.** intelligent
    **b.** coordinated
    **c.** responsive and interactive
    **d.** entertaining

A

c. Your feelings of connection to your baby will deepen as she becomes more **responsive and interactive.**

Okay, so your feelings of attachment to her are growing, but when will she start feeling the same way toward you? The answer is right about now. Your baby has developed the mental capacity to associate you with satisfying her needs and wants, and can summon up a mental image of you to keep her company if you're not physically there.

There are _____ types of attachment relationships between parents and children.

    **a.** 4
    **b.** 6
    **c.** 2
    **d.** 5

c. There are **2** types of attachment relationships between parents and children.

The two main types are (1) *secure*, meaning that the child feels confident that the parent will respond appropriately to his needs; and (2) *insecure*, meaning that the child is constantly afraid that his needs won't be met by the parent.

_____

If you and your baby haven't
formed a strong attachment yet,
it's ____ too late.

- **a.** not
- **b.** already
- **c.** almost
- **d.** way

A

a. If you and your baby haven't formed a strong attachment yet, it's **not** too late.

When it comes to forming an attachment to your baby, the younger she is the better. But if, for example, you were in the military and just returned from deployment, it's by no means too late.

TIP Just jump in now and do as much as you can. But be patient—with her and yourself. Besides investing time, the way you react and respond to your baby will have a great influence on the kind of attachment you and she eventually form.

Girls with strong attachments to their father are less likely to become _____ early.

    **a.** independent
    **b.** self-sufficient
    **c.** sexually active
    **d.** romantically involved

c.  Girls with strong attachments to their father are
less likely to become **sexu-
ally active** early.

It's way too early to be worrying
about this, but girls who have
strong relationships with their
father enter puberty later, are
less likely to get involved with
drugs or alcohol, and are less
likely to become teen mothers.

For new parents, the number one stressor is _____ .

    **a.** money
    **b.** lack of sex
    **c.** division of labor
    **d.** washing dishes

c. For new parents, the number one stressor is **division of labor**.

Before the baby comes, most couples say they want to divide things up equally. But when reality sets in, they often slip into "traditional" gender roles.

———

TIP Talk with your partner about what "equal" means. It doesn't mean that you change 6 diapers a day and she does the other 6. Instead, calculate how much time it takes for each task that needs to be done and divide things up so that you're each putting in the same amount of time.

The one toy that's essential for every nursery is _____ .

    **a.** a cell phone
    **b.** a rocking horse
    **c.** blocks
    **d.** a gerbil

A

c. The one toy that's essential for every nursery is **blocks**.

There are dozens of high-tech toys and games that claim to be essential to your child's physical and mental development. Some are worthwhile; others are a waste of time and money. But blocks—just about the lowest-tech thing of all—truly are essential.

TIP Playing with blocks helps your baby develop a range of physical and cognitive skills, including hand-eye coordination, grasping and releasing, and size and pattern identification.

_____ with your baby is just as important as feeding and diaper changing.

**a.** Sleeping
**b.** Playing
**c.** Walking
**d.** Talking

A

b. **Playing with** your baby is just important as feeding and diaper changing.

Children who don't have much chance to play suffer in a variety of ways, including intellectually. Babies who play—especially with their dad—are more empathetic, manage their emotions better, are more social, are more persistent when working on challenging tasks, and have higher IQs.

TIP One of your goals should be to expose your baby to the most varied, enriching play environment possible.

---

Fathers often treat \_\_\_\_\_ differently.

    **a.** boys and girls
    **b.** cats and dogs
    **c.** fish and mice
    **d.** mac and cheese

a. Fathers often treat **boys and girls** differently.

Fathers tend to vocalize more with infant sons than daughters. They're also more rough-and-tumble with boys than with girls, and are a little less likely to hug or snuggle with a boy than a girl. Dads also are more encouraging of their sons' quests for independence and they'll respond more quickly to a crying girl than a crying boy. Mothers are somewhat better at treating boys and girls the same, but they too are more responsive to crying girls than boys.

Don't discourage _____ from playing with dolls, or _____ from playing with trucks.

a. boys, girls
b. girls, boys
c. dogs, cats
d. men, women

A

a. Don't discourage **boys** from playing with dolls, or **girls** from playing with trucks.

If you have a boy, teach him that asking for help can be good, and that it's okay to express emotions. If you have a girl, encourage her to play physically and teach her that assertiveness isn't unfeminine.

TIP Don't force your child into behavior that doesn't fit with his or her character and temperament. Sometimes boys will be boys and girls will be girls—just as the old stereotypes tell us. And that's not a bad thing.

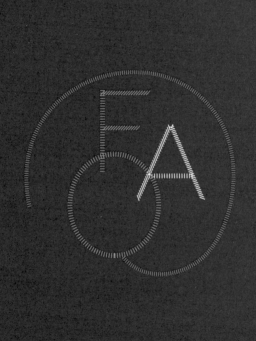

Your baby is now able to _____
on his own.

    **a.** walk
    **b.** play blackjack
    **c.** stand
    **d.** sleep

c. Your baby is now able to **stand** on his own.

He moves easily from crawling to sitting and may even be able to pull himself upright. Once there, he can stand with very little support—and may even try a few seconds without any support at all.

If you hold her hand, your baby will _____ .

    **a.** climb the stairs
    **b.** cross the road
    **c.** start dancing
    **d.** walk anywhere

# A

d. If you hold her hand, your baby will **walk anywhere**.

If you hold her hand, she'll walk for miles. And if you don't hold her hand, she's perfecty capable of "cruising" (walking—usually sideways—holding onto or leaning up against something for support) anywhere she wants.

Your baby may now be using one ＿＿＿ more than the other.

- **a.** hand or foot
- **b.** bathroom
- **c.** television station
- **d.** set of silverware

# A

a. Your baby may now be using one **hand or foot** more than the other.

He's discovering that he can control each side of his body separately, and he may be exhibiting a "handedness" preference. He may, for example, use one hand for picking up, the other for manipulating things.

TIP Encourage him to use both hands to do things, but respect his preference for one over the other.

As her _____ improves, she's getting more persistent.

   **a.** coordination
   **b.** singing voice
   **c.** memory
   **d.** math ability

A

---

c.  As her **memory** improves, she's getting more persistent.

It's harder than it used to be to distract her from whatever she's doing. If you do manage to turn her attention to something else, she'll go right back to her original activity as soon as you quit bugging her.

Your baby now understands the
\_\_\_\_\_ he's been using.

    **a.** apps
    **b.** meaning of the words
    **c.** tools
    **d.** camera

A

b. Your baby now understands the **meaning of the words** he's been using.

Although he's been saying "dada" and "mama" for a while, he probably didn't know what they meant. Now he does, and he'll use them—and a few others, like "no" and "bye-bye," deliberately and correctly.

Many single women find men who are active in their children's lives ____ .

   **a.** effeminate
   **b.** amusing
   **c.** attractive
   **d.** threatening

c. Many single women find men who are active in their children's lives **attractive**.

For a lot of women, there's apparently something irresistible about a man playing happily with a child. A man with a child and a dog is even better.

———

TIP If you're a single father, enjoy it. If you're married or are in a serious relationship and want to stay that way, watch out.

If your baby isn't _____ to the music, don't turn it off.

    **a.** dancing
    **b.** singing along
    **c.** paying attention
    **d.** tapping her foot

c. If your baby isn't **paying attention** to the music, don't turn it off.

Just because your baby doesn't seem to be paying attention, doesn't mean he's not listening. In fact, research shows that babies get just as much out of it when we think they aren't paying attention as when we think they are. (Clearly, we're getting something wrong.)

TIP If you want to try to refocus his attention, try changing to a song you know he really likes.

Keep talking to your baby—even if she _____ .

    **a.** makes faces at you
    **b.** doesn't respond
    **c.** throws things at you
    **d.** doesn't get your jokes

b. Keep talking to your baby—even if she **doesn't respond**.

Your baby can't hold up her end of the conversation, but don't stop talking to her. In fact, the more you talk, the more she'll learn.

---

TIP Encourage and expand. If your baby says "ba ba," don't just leave it at that. Instead, respond with a full sentence, something like, "Do you want your bottle?" or "Yes, that is a sheep" (depending on what you think she means by "ba ba").

Ask your baby questions that she can respond to by _____ .

**a.** laughing
**b.** crying
**c.** answering verbally
**d.** pointing

A

d. Ask your baby questions that she can respond to by pointing.

If your baby doesn't seem too interested in using words, you can still engage her in conversations by asking questions that allow her to show you the answer instead of saying it. Things like, "Where's your tummy?" If she points to the right place, cheer. If not, point it out for her ("Here's your tummy!") and ask another question. Or point to her nose instead. Chances are she'll get a good giggle out of that.

Try to cut back on using _____ .

    **a.** exotic spices
    **b.** sarcasm
    **c.** "no" and "don't"
    **d.** profanity

c. Try to cut back on using "no" and "don't."

First of all, "no" and "don't" are too broad. If he's holding a knife and you shout "no," it's not clear whether you mean for him to put down the knife, use a spoon instead, or take a nap. And "no" and "don't" discourage creativity and exploration, too.

TIP Explanations like "knives are sharp and can hurt you" help him better understand what, exactly, he's doing wrong.

Boys who get cuddled a lot have
_____ than boys who don't.

    **a.** higher pain tolerance
    **b.** more docile personalities
    **c.** more independence
    **d.** higher IQs

# A

d. Boys who get cuddled a lot have **higher IQs** than boys who don't.

We have a tendency to treat boys and girls differently from the day they're born. Researchers had two groups of people watch a child play with a jack-in-the-box. One group was told they were watching a girl, the other was told they were watching a boy. When the jack popped up, the girl group described "her" as being scared. The boy group said "he" was angry. Most people would be more likely to cuddle a scared child than an angry one.

Your baby may decide to _____
by clinging and crying at the
same time.

    **a.** annoy you
    **b.** entertain you
    **c.** punish you
    **d.** make you cry

A

c. Your baby may decide to **punish you** by clinging and crying at the same time.

As she becomes more sensitive to your emotions, she's also getting better at expressing her own. For example, if you leave her alone for longer than she'd like (only she knows what that means), you may witness the not-uncommon contradictory behavior described above.

TIP This is the only way she knows to express these feelings. Enjoy it while it lasts. In a few years she'll switch to slamming doors and shouting "I hate you."

Your baby may now be able to
_____ from a squatting position.

    **a.** sit
    **b.** stand
    **c.** cry
    **d.** poop

A

b. Your baby may now be able to **stand** from a squatting position.

Your baby can get himself to a standing position by straightening his legs and pushing off with his hands. He may even be able to squat back down if there's something down there that's important enough for him to pick up.

Your baby can now _____ using only the railing for assistance.

**a.** run
**b.** potty
**c.** climb stairs
**d.** play the piano

A

c. Your baby can now **climb stairs** using only the railing for assistance.

When walking with you, she likes to show off by holding on to only one of your hands. To add to the degree of difficulty, she'll often want to hold on to a toy or something else in her other hand.

Your baby probably adores _____ with you.

    **a.** quiet play
    **b.** watching reality TV
    **c.** arguing
    **d.** rough play

d. Your baby probably adores **rough play** with you.

Whether you've got a boy or a girl, most babies this age love any kind of physical play, such as being hung upside down, bouncing on your knee, rolling around, and wrestling with you.

———

TIP Although your baby may like to play rough, he's still a baby. So be careful. And pay attention to his cues. If he starts fussing or seems unhappy, stop right away. If playing with you scares him, he's not going to want to do it.

Your baby can now _____ a spoon pretty well, but prefers using her hands.

**a.** operate
**b.** throw
**c.** chew on
**d.** scratch her back with

# A

a. Your baby can now **operate** a spoon pretty well, but prefers using her hands.

Spoons are great, but your baby may feel that she can't get as much food into her mouth as quickly as she wants to. So if she's really hungry, she'll go back to using her hands.

---

TIP Always have a spoon available anyway. Eventually, she'll start using it as her primary tool.

Your baby can hold a crayon and
will draw _____ .

    **a.** on anything he can reach
    **b.** between the lines
    **c.** incorrect conclusions
    **d.** Picasso knock-offs

# A

a. Your baby can hold a crayon and will draw on anything he can reach.

Your little artist sees the world as his canvas, meaning that everything is fair game—walls, windows, books, floors, pets, siblings, himself, and occasionally even a piece of paper.

TIP If he wears clothes with pockets, check them for crayons before throwing them in the laundry.

At some point during this month, your baby will learn that she can _____ a chair.

    **a.** poop in
    **b.** sit in
    **c.** draw on
    **d.** move

d. At some point during this month, your baby will learn that she can **move** a chair.

One day, your baby will lean against a chair and accidentally make it move a little. She'll immediately understand that she's the one responsible, and will do it again. And again. She may spend the rest of the day (and the month) shoving that chair around the house.

TIP Do another round of child-proofing, this time looking for things that can be damaged by having a chair slam into them.

Your baby is already establishing his own _____ .

    **a.** credit
    **b.** home
    **c.** independence
    **d.** sexual identity

A

---

d.  Your baby is already establishing his own **sexual identity**.

If you've got a girl, your baby may start identifying with her mother and other females and want to do what they do. If you've got a boy, he may identify with you and other males and want to do what you do. That said, your baby is still very young and his or her sexual identity isn't fully formed. So if your daughter acts more like a boy or your son acts like a girl, you're not necessarily seeing the future. But if you are, that's OK, too.

His vocabulary is growing, but he can't _____ .

   **a.** put together sentences
   **b.** spell
   **c.** use the phone
   **d.** write

# A

a. His vocabulary is growing, but he can't **put together sentences**.

But he'll babble in long paragraphs—sometimes to himself if he can't find an audience—tossing in a recognizable word now and then.

Your baby has mastered the art of _____ .

    **a.** asking for candy
    **b.** calligraphy
    **c.** ignoring you
    **d.** laughing at you

c. Your baby has mastered the art of **ignoring you**.

She's developed an incredible ability to hear what she wants to. She'll completely ignore a shouted "Get away from that stove!" but will stop whatever she's doing and rush to your side if you whisper "ice cream" from another zip code.

Besides happiness and sadness, your baby is now capable of sophisticated emotions, such as _____ .

**a.** jealousy
**b.** boredom
**c.** lying
**d.** disappointment

# A

a. Besides happiness and sadness, your baby is now capable of sophisticated emotions, such as **jealousy**.

If you play with another baby, for example, he'll protest loudly. He's also getting much more demonstrative and will show genuine tenderness toward you and his stuffed animals.

TIP If you do need to pay attention to another baby, make sure to spend an equal amount of time with yours.

Your baby is content to play alongside other children, but he's not ready to _____ .

    **a.** play with them
    **b.** play alone
    **c.** play with the family pet
    **d.** play hockey

a. Your baby is content to play alongside other children, but he's not ready to **play with them**.

At this age, babies generally play next to other children, not with them. Cooperative play won't start happening for at least another few months, maybe longer.

———

TIP If your baby and another child are playing next to each other, pay attention. Babies are still learning about cause and effect and may ask themselves, "What would happen if I poke that other kid in the eye?"

---

If your baby is having trouble
eating or _____ food, call the
pediatrician immediately.

    **a.** swallowing
    **b.** throwing
    **c.** drawing with
    **d.** ignoring

A

a. If your baby is having trouble eating or **swallowing** food, call the pediatrician immediately.

Besides resulting in nutritional deficiencies and general health problems, having trouble eating may interfere with your baby's use of her jaws, lips, and tongue, and may even have an impact on cognitive and language skills.

TIP If you're worried something may be wrong with your baby, call the doctor. Finding out it was really no big deal is far better than ignoring something and finding out later that it was serious.

Your gut reactions about your child's health are usually _____ .

    **a.** pretty accurate
    **b.** completely wrong
    **c.** silly
    **d.** nothing to worry about

A

a. Your gut reactions about your child's health are usually **pretty accurate**.

You may not be the most experienced parent on the planet, but your gut instincts about what ails your child are usually pretty good, and should be acted upon.

TIP This doesn't mean you should take your child to the emergency room for every sniffle or sneeze, but there's nothing wrong with calling up your pediatrician's 24-hour advice line. After all, that's what you and your insurance company are paying for.

For airplane travel, always be sure to bring something for the baby to _____ .

**a.** suck on
**b.** throw at passengers
**c.** read
**d.** cuddle with

# A

a. For airplane travel, always be sure to bring something for the baby to **suck on**.

On the way up and on the way down, every child under 2 years of age should suck on something—breast, bottle, or pacifier. This will counteract the cabin pressurization and reduce the chances of painful earaches. It may also make the baby a little drowsier.

Always bring _____ when travel-
ing with a child.

    **a.** a nanny
    **b.** antacid
    **c.** a first-aid kit
    **d.** a leash

c. Always bring **a first-aid kit** when traveling with a child.

Children—especially tired ones—always seem to be getting hurt. Having a basic first-aid kit on hand will allow you to treat minor bumps and bruises without having to find a pharmacy in an unfamiliar city or country.

TIP Always have lots of Band-Aids. You many not even be able to see what's bothering your child, but Band-Aids almost always seem to help (especially if the "injury" is just a way of asking for some attention).

For short car trips, leaving _____ will ensure quieter travel and a happier baby.

    **a.** an hour before naptime
    **b.** first thing in the morning
    **c.** at bedtime
    **d.** on weekends

a. For short car trips, leaving **an hour before naptime** will ensure quieter travel and a happier baby.

Car travel tends to knock babies out, and if you drive as far as you can while yours is asleep, you'll probably get pretty far.

———

TIP Get a travel pillow for your baby and put it around his neck when you first get in the car. Having his head supported could make his nap last a bit longer.

Along with all your expenses and responsibilities, it's important to think about _____ .

**a.** a new house
**b.** life insurance
**c.** running away
**d.** divorce

b. Along with all your expenses and responsibilities, it's important to think about **life insurance**.

Having a child may make you want to live forever and not miss a single second with your child. But it also makes you confront your own mortality. Life insurance comes in two basic flavors: term and cash value.

TIP If you're not familiar with the ins and outs of insurance and the advantages and disadvantages of each of your options, get some advice from a financial adviser.

For plane travel, buy your baby her own _____ .

   **a.** pony
   **b.** diapers
   **c.** seat
   **d.** oxygen mask

c. For plane travel, buy your baby her own **seat**.

Yes, it's more expensive, but holding your baby on your lap for hours—especially in a packed plane—can be a real pain. It's also not nearly as safe as having the baby secured in her own car seat.

TIP Because airlines occasionally offer discounted seats for infants, this may be one of those times where it's better to make your reservation by phone than online.

If your employer offers long-term disability coverage, _____ .

    **a.** skip it
    **b.** sign up now
    **c.** call the police
    **d.** consider it

b. If your employer offers long-term disability coverage, **sign up now**.

Take a long, hard look at disability coverage. A long-term disability can sometimes be more devastating to your family's finances than death.

———

TIP If your employer doesn't offer this kind of coverage or you're self-employed, talk with your insurance broker. Many long-term disability plans have a waiting period of as long as several months before benefits kick in. If so, consider a short-term policy too, to cover the gap.

Your baby's favorite mode of transportation is still _____ .

    **a.** magic carpet
    **b.** crawling
    **c.** being carried
    **d.** running

b. Your baby's favorite mode of transportation is still **crawling**.

Your little one may be able to take a few unassisted steps this month, but he'll still rely on crawling or scooting to get from place to place, mostly because it's faster.

Your baby has an active vocabulary of _____ real words and the same number of sound words.

   **a.** 6 to 8
   **b.** 200
   **c.** 3
   **d.** thousands

# A

a. Your baby has a vocabulary of **6 to 8** real words and the same number of sound words.

Sound words (*moo, woof, boom,* and so on) are among her favorites. Her passive vocabulary (words she understands but can't say) may be as large as 50 words, and she'll gleefully identify many of her body parts as well as other familiar objects, such as you, Mom, her bottle, her crib, shoes, and the family pets.

Your baby _____ almost anything anyone does.

    **a.** laughs at
    **b.** ignores
    **c.** imitates
    **d.** tweets about

c. Your baby **imitates** almost anything anyone does.

Your baby wants to be just like you, and as long as you're doing it, she'll love sweeping the floor, typing on the computer, texting, talking on the phone, howling in pain if you hurt yourself, and even spitting out curse words. Watch your mouth.

His sense of _____ is developing quickly.

    **a.** humor
    **b.** smell
    **c.** indignation
    **d.** fair play

a. His sense of **humor** is developing quickly.

He finds incongruities enormously entertaining. If you tell him a dog says "moo," crawl around and act like a baby, or pretend to eat your phone, he'll laugh hysterically.

Your baby is most likely to play and socialize with other children when she's _____ .

    **a.** at the park
    **b.** at home
    **c.** at grandma's house
    **d.** in the middle of the street

b. Your baby is most likely to play and socialize with other children when she's **at home**.

Your baby is more willing to play with others where she feels most secure—and that's most likely in your own home. In less-secure environments, though, she's not nearly as sociable and won't stray too far from you.

One of the best ways to cope with anger at your child is to _____ .

**a.** run away forever
**b.** break an expensive vase
**c.** spank him
**d.** laugh

A

d. One of the best ways to cope with anger at your child is to **laugh**.

Babies are hardwired to make us angry—it's part of their normal development. That's one of the ways they learn about limits. It's not always easy (in fact, it's usually pretty hard), but try to see the humor in situations that might otherwise make you angry. For example, while it's a pain to clean up, writing on the wall with lipstick is pretty funny—if you let it be.

If there is no physical reason for your baby to be pitching a tantrum, it's best to _____ .

    **a.** scream at him
    **b.** give him what he wants
    **c.** ignore him
    **d.** bribe him to stop

c. If there is no physical reason for your baby to be pitching a tantrum, it's best to **ignore him**.

When your baby throws a tantrum, try to figure out what's wrong: Is he frustrated at not being able to get you to understand something? Is he angry that you're not giving him what he wants? Is he in some kind of pain?

TIP If there are no bumps, bruises, cuts, or any other physical explanations, ignore him. If your child has a tantrum in a public place, just pick him up and carry him out.

When enforcing rules, it's important to be _____ .

    **a.** consistent
    **b.** inconsistent
    **c.** harsh
    **d.** critical

A

a. When enforcing rules, it's important to be **consistent**.

Don't allow certain kinds of behavior one day and then turn around and forbid the same behavior another day. That'll just confuse your child and will increase the likelihood that he'll get himself into trouble.

Limit the number of _____
you give before imposing
consequences.

    **a.** hot dogs
    **b.** warnings
    **c.** spankings
    **d.** directions

b. Limit the number of **warnings** you give before imposing consequences.

If you tell your baby "No" five times, give two "If-you-do-that-one-more-time" warnings, and three "final" warnings, you've just taught your baby that it's okay to ignore you at least nine times.

_____ use the TV/DVD/tablet as an electronic babysitter.

    **a.** Always
    **b.** Frequently
    **c.** Try not to
    **d.** Joyfully

c. **Try not to** use the TV/DVD/
tablet as an electronic
babysitter.

Children under 3 spend an
average of 3 hours every day in
front of one electronic screen
or another. And most of the
programming they're exposed to
isn't age-appropriate.

TIP Ideally, you wouldn't put your
child in front of a screen until age
2 or 3. But sometimes we need
to take a phone call or a quick
shower. Stay away from "educa-
tional" videos—the more time
babies spend watching them, the
smaller their vocabularies.

If your baby is pounding on a glass window with a hammer, _____ .

**a.** calmly disarm her
**b.** scream at her
**c.** take a picture
**d.** throw something at her

# A

a.  If your baby is pounding on a glass window with a hammer, **calmly disarm her**.

Stop dangerous behavior quickly, but subtly. If you scream, drop your coffee, and leap over the living room furniture to wrestle her to the ground, she'll find your reaction so much fun that she'll repeat what she did to provoke it in the first place. Instead, tell her to stop banging. If that doesn't work, calmly walk over and give her something softer.

Your baby genius is now using
_____ to solve problems and
overcome obstacles.

  **a.** magic
  **b.** trial and error
  **c.** manipulation
  **d.** begging

b. Your baby genius is now using **trial and error** to solve problems and overcome obstacles.

In a major intellectual leap, when confronted by a difficult challenge, your baby will make a number of attempts to solve it instead of either giving up or pestering you to do it for him.

_____ babies this age pinch, hit, and/or bite strangers, family, even animals.

    **a.** No
    **b.** Twenty-five percent of
    **c.** Angry
    **d.** Most

d. **Most** babies this age pinch, hit, and/or bite strangers, family, even animals.

Right around their first birthdays, most babies go through a physically aggressive phase. Fortunately, it usually lasts only a few months. (Although when you're being bitten a few times every day, that can seem like a really long time.)

_____ for too long contributes to ear infections and/or tooth decay.

   **a.** Bottle-feeding
   **b.** Breast-feeding
   **c.** Using a pacifier
   **d.** Drinking fruit juices

A

a. **Bottle-feeding** for too long contributes to ear infections and/or tooth decay.

Bottle-fed babies are more susceptible to ear infections and tooth decay. Babies often drink from bottles while on their back, and liquid drips out of bottles without the baby having to suck. As a result, milk can pool in the baby's mouth, back up into the eustachian tubes, and cause ear infections. Also, soaking teeth in milk increases the risk of decay. Breast-fed babies are rarely on their backs when they eat, and the mouth is usually emptied with every swallow.

Your partner may continue breast-feeding the baby after 12 months because _____ .

   **a.** it annoys you
   **b.** she and the baby like it
   **c.** she gets paid to do it
   **d.** it's politically correct

b. Your partner may continue breast-feeding the baby after 12 months because **she and the baby like it.**

There's nothing wrong with continuing limited breast-feeding if your baby and partner both enjoy it. Both of them may really like the contact and connection with each other. But at this point, it's providing your baby with much more emotional sustenance than nutrition.

When transitioning baby from breast to bottle, cut out \_\_\_\_\_ feeding(s) first.

    **a.** the morning
    **b.** the midday
    **c.** the evening
    **d.** all

# A

b. When transitioning baby from breast-feeding the bottles, cut out **the midday feeding(s) first.**

Phase out the breast gradually. Since babies are usually most attached to morning and evening feedings, start by eliminating the midday feedings and replacing them with a bottle, some solid food, or both.

---

TIP If that goes well, drop the morning feeding next.

---

Don't start your baby on cow's milk until after _____ .

    **a.** a solar eclipse
    **b.** her first birthday
    **c.** high school
    **d.** she eats her vegetables

A

---

b. Don't start your baby on cow's milk until after **her first birthday**.

Pediatricians recommend that babies drink whole milk, as the fat in the milk is important for healthy brain development. Talk to your pediatrician before switching to a lower-fat milk.

Your baby's first birthday party is much more _____ .

    **a.** expensive than you'd think
    **b.** for her than for you
    **c.** for you than for her
    **d.** entertaining than a movie

c. Your baby's first birthday party is much more **for you than for her**.

Still, it's a pretty big milestone.

---

TIP **Keep it small (2–3 kids at most) and skip the clowns (too scary for most babies). After the guests have gone, pop open a bottle of champagne with your partner and celebrate. In many ways, you've grown and developed as much as your baby has. And you've gone from being so tentative and worried that you wouldn't know what to do, to confident and competent. Happy birthday!**

# RESOURCES

Here are just a few resources to get you
pointed in the right direction. You'll find a
much more comprehensive list at mrdad.
com/resources. If you know of a resource—
or category of resources—that can benefit
dads and their families, let us know:
armin@mrdad.com

## GENERAL

KIDSINTHEHOUSE.COM features 8,000
videos (including several dozen of mine)
from more than 400 experts that can help
answer all your questions on pregnancy and
parenting. www.kidsinthehouse.com

PREGNANCYMAGAZINE.COM is one of the
leading pregnancy websites. They publish
11 issues per year—including "The Pregnant
Dad," the only pregnancy magazine issue
written and edited by new and experienced
fathers. www.pregnancymagazine.com

## FATHERHOOD

CITY DADS GROUP is a growing, national
organization dedicated to helping fathers
socialize and support one another. www.
citydadsgroup.com

JUST A DAD 247 has an amazingly comprehensive map of dads' groups all around the world—not just at-home dad groups, but all of them. www.justadad247.com/map-of-dad-groups

MRDAD.COM is my website. You can get information there about pretty much every aspect of pregnancy, childbirth, and fatherhood; find out more about my other fatherhood books; and send me questions and comments. www.mrdad.com

NATIONAL AT-HOME DAD NETWORK has great resources on how to find/register/start a dads' group. They also have links to stay-at-home dad bloggers, statistics, resources, and a lot more.www.athomedad.org

## FINANCES

COLLEGE SAVINGS PLAN NETWORK offers great info on all of the state-sponsored college savings plans and referrals to the one in your state. www.collegesavings.org

FINANCIAL PLANNING ASSOCIATION provides information on financial planning and referrals to certified financial planners in your area. www.plannersearch.org/Pages/home.aspx

**FAMILIES AND WORK INSTITUTE** is a research and advocacy organization that produces a wealth of resources for working families and employers.
www.familiesandwork.org

**HEALTHY CHILDREN** is sponsored by the American Academy of Pediatrics for parents. It provides formation on topics including child development, health, safety, and family issues.
www.healthychildren.org

**IMMUNIZATION ACTION COALITION** provides the nation's premier source of child, teen, and adult immunization information for health professionals and their patients. Tel: (651) 647-9009 www.immunize.org

**LA LECHE LEAGUE INTERNATIONAL** provides information and mother-to-mother support through La Leche League's network of lay leaders and professional experts.
www.lalecheleague.org

**MY CHILD WITHOUT LIMITS** offers information on a variety of disorders that can cause developmental learning delays, including Down syndrome, epilepsy, and hearing and vision impairments. The online community offers an opportunity for families to connect and share words of encouragement and to provide solutions to everyday problems. www.mychildwithoutlimits.org

NATIONAL HIGHWAY TRAFFIC SAFETY ADMINISTRATION offers the latest info on car and car-seat safety. Includes a shopping guide for car seats, recall information, and safety literature.www.nhtsa.gov

## HEALTH

POSTPARTUM DADS www.postpartumdads.org

POSTPARTUM SUPPORT INTERNATIONAL is dedicated to helping women suffering from perinatal mood and anxiety disorders, including postpartum depression, the most common complication of childbirth. www.postpartum.net

PREEMIE BABIES 101 is a parent blog inspired by the many diverse experiences that are common to parents of preemies. www.preemiebabies101.com

**ARMIN A. BROTT**, Mr. Dad, is a nationally recognized expert on parenting and the author of eight books on fatherhood, including the best-selling *The New Father: A Dad's Guide to the First Year* and *The Expectant Father: The Ultimate Guide for Dads-to-Be*. He has also written on parenting for the *New York Times Magazine*, the *Washington Post*, *Sports Illustrated*, and *Newsweek*, among many other publications, and he has been a speaker at the Dad 2.0 Summit. He writes the popular nationally syndicated column "Ask Mr. Dad" and hosts "Positive Parenting," a weekly syndicated talk show. Brott lives with his family in Oakland, California. To learn more, visit his website: www.mr.dad.com.

Please also connect with us on social media:

@mrdad

Facebook.com/mrdad

Pinterest.com/mrdad

Linkedin.com/in/mrdad

plus.google.com/+Mrdad